Preach it!

Preach it!

Understanding African Caribbean Preaching

Carol Tomlin

scm press

First published in 2019 by the SCM Press Norwich
Editorial office
3rd Floor, Invicta House
108–114 Golden Lane
London EC1Y 0TG, UK

www.scmpress.co.uk

SCM Press is an imprint of Hymns Ancient & Modern Ltd
(a registered charity)

Hymns Ancient & Modern® is a registered trademark of
Hymns Ancient & Modern Ltd
13A Hellesdon Park Road, Norwich,
Norfolk NR6 5DR, UK

British Library Cataloguing in Publication data

A catalogue record for this book is available
from the British Library

978 0 334 05737 6

Typeset by Regent Typesetting Ltd
Printed and bound in Great Britain by
CPI Group (UK) Ltd

Contents

Acknowledgements

I would like to express my thanks and acknowledge the many African Caribbean Pentecostal preachers whose sermons inform this book and who are a constant source of inspiration. I am especially grateful for the sermons of Pastor Nathan Turner and Pastor Esther Bonsu that are printed in the Appendix, and to Pastor Mark Liburd whose comments have been invaluable. I wish to thank my family, Sylvie (my mother), Beryl, Tony and cousin Donna for their love, support and encouragement. I would like to thank my co-pastor Prophetess Tamika and her daughter Kirai for being my extended family and my dear friends Sharon, Funke, Sylvie, Pamela, Joy, Moureen and Dr Prophet Oscar. Thank you to my church family, Restoration Fellowship Ministries. I have welcomed your prayers throughout this project. My appreciation extends to my Lord and Saviour Jesus Christ who gave me the ideas for this book.

Acknowledgments

Preface

The royal wedding of Prince Harry to Meghan Markle on Saturday 19 May 2018 gave the worldwide audience a glimpse of the preaching of Bishop Michael Curry, the presiding Episcopal bishop who 'stole the show'. He demonstrated a presentation of preaching that I have observed throughout my life. Although the bishop is certainly not Pentecostal, his style of preaching on that wonderful day is reminiscent of African Caribbean Pentecostal preaching, the subject of this book.

My fascination with African Caribbean preaching began when I was ten, as far as I can recall. I attended and subsequently became a member of the New Testament Church of God in Leeds, West Yorkshire. I vividly remember the 'mothers' of the church and that one dared not move but had to sit still in 'big people' church, especially during the 'Word'. Amazingly, I was able to sit unmoved for an hour or more and listen to the most dynamically stylized preaching. I was spellbound by the sermons of Pastor Terence Caine and others, who preached at the district conventions and building programmes (a fund-raising event). I can still remember when I was 15 years old, the title and some of the content of a sermon by Pastor Grey entitled: 'What time is it? [long pause] End time'. In those days much of the preaching along with the songs were eschatological in nature. Oh how times have changed! Thankfully, the style remains the same. To this day I am mesmerized by what I have referred to in my earlier research as 'black preaching style'. I believe that God had planted the seed of interest in this art of preaching in my soul and mind.

It is not coincidental that my parents were from the Windrush generation, the Caribbean migrants who settled in

Britain during the post-war period. It is not accidental that I was captivated by the sounds, vibrancy and eloquence of my parents and older relatives. Coming from Clarendon, Jamaica they retained in their speech much of the basilect features, the Jamaican language/dialect furthest removed from Standard English. When they communicated with each other, I would at times roll around in peals of laughter at their incredible sense of humour and even when my mother reprimanded me her words sounded almost like poetry.

Back to the African Caribbean Pentecostal preaching which is contextual and reflects the language of the community. I have observed in the twenty-first century that the style of preaching among African diasporans from the Pentecostal/Charismatic tradition is similar in diverse geographical locations. I have had the privilege of attending at various points in my life the following types of churches with varied cultural compositions. These include Pentecostal churches with predominantly African Caribbean people; one whose congregants are primarily West African; an evangelical church with an ethnically mixed congregation, and a Charismatic-type African Episcopal church where the congregants are mainly African American. Much of the material for this book is not only based on extensive in-depth research conducted over 35 years, but also my own lived-in experience of preaching for almost two decades. I am an insider, not gazing through the window as a stranger; my heart and passion intertwined with discovering more about the preached word of my heritage. I am a minister who co-founded an independent non-denominational church, Restoration Fellowship Ministries, which presently has two branches, one in Birmingham and the other in Leeds.

Part of the journey to this book took place during my undergraduate days as a student teacher working with Professor Viv Edwards, and subsequent postgraduate and postdoctoral studies. As previously mentioned, God had planted the seed, and it had germinated in my first book, *Black Language Style in Sacred and Secular Contexts*. The seed has further grown in the form of this present book, which I hope will be of interest to clergy across Christian denominations and to those in the fields of homiletics, linguistics, communication and anthropology. It should benefit anyone interested in the spoken art of preaching.

Introduction

The aim of this book is to examine the discursive practices of African Caribbean Pentecostal preaching in Britain. It explores the origins of modern Pentecostalism emanating from North America and its African roots. The North American narrative provides a context for the transportation of Pentecostalism from the Caribbean to Britain and discussion of the theologies and liturgy of African Caribbean Pentecostalism. The linguistic components of sermons or homilies reflecting the communicative patterns of African diasporans are documented. The book proposes a hermeneutical frame for African Caribbean preaching resonating with aspects of global Pentecostalism but with distinguishing features. The ideas discussed throughout this book lend support to the notion that African Caribbean Pentecostals have inherited underlying elements of West African languages and religious practices, still very much in evidence in contemporary diasporic communities such as Britain. It is recognized, as Ackah (2017) suggests, that African and diasporic communities are dynamic and diverse and a number of forces such as enslavement, colonialism and globalisation have shaped the religious expressions of the people; however, an African ontology remains. Therefore, as a point of reference, the term *black* as a prefix will be used generically to refer to the cultures, languages and more specifically to the preaching of people of African descent in diverse geographical locations, despite objections to the term by some scholars (for instance, see Olofinjana, 2017, p. xvi).

African Caribbean churches and preaching

It is relevant at this point to briefly explain that African Caribbean churches are a part of what are currently referred to in Britain as black majority churches (BMCs). These churches tend to be Pentecostal or Charismatic and delineated by two groups: the first comprises congregants predominantly from an African background, the second, Caribbean, also referred to as African Caribbean. Though similar in some respects, the latter generally has a longer history in Britain both ecclesiastically and in academic texts. Recent scholarly writing in the field of African Caribbean Pentecostal churches can be seen, for instance, in the work of Beckford (2000, 2013); Aldred (2005, 2010); Adedibu (2012); Reddie (2014) and Muir (2015). However, the hermeneutical framework for preaching in these churches are relatively under-researched (Mullings, 2007, 2010).

The literature on 'black preaching' tends to emanate from North America where the cultural context and the denominational affiliations are rather different though there are some similarities in the style of preaching (see for instance, Mitchell 1970, 1990; LaRue 2011, 2016 and Thomas 2016). Academic writing on the strategies for preaching in African Caribbean Pentecostal churches is extremely sparse, drawing primarily on early studies by Sutcliff and Tomlin (1986) and research conducted by Tomlin (1988, 1999, 2014). There are generalist books dealing with preaching, advocating a somewhat narrow Eurocentric homiletic tradition (Gilbert, 2011; Stevenson, 2017). Yet Christianity, especially Pentecostalism, is growing rapidly in the global South, and reports of the decline in church attendance in several mainline British churches is parallel in recent decades to an upsurge in church planting among leaders of black majority, Asian and Latin American churches (Goodhew 2012; Olofinjana 2017). The act of preaching has been pivotal to their expansion, and theories in homiletics should inculcate the multi-identities of the carriers of Christianity. African Caribbean Pentecostal preaching is well placed as a starting point to traverse this terrain. It is first necessary to provide the context for this preaching by focusing on the origins of the African diaspora and the worldview.

The origins of the African diaspora: African worldview and orality

The origins of the common linguistic cultural heritage of African diasporan communities lie in the system of slavery, the institution responsible for the spread of Africans in the New World. During the enslavement period from the nineteenth century, the slaves were systematically separated from their respective linguistic and ethnic groups. Hundreds of years saw the evolution of several different societies with many political organizations, cultures and different languages (Zeleza 2006).

The marked differences in African societies have been cited to demonstrate the obstacles African slaves in the New World faced in maintaining aspects of their traditional cultures and languages. Despite these differences, there appear to be some underlying similarities, certainly in West Africa, the landmass from which many of the slaves came. Redfield (1953 cited in Levine 1977, p. 4) chooses to discuss these fundamental commonalities under the umbrella 'style of life'. As Levine (1977, p. 4) further comments:

> Though they varied widely in language, institutions, gods, and familial patterns, they shared a fundamental outlook toward the past, present, and future and common means of cultural expression, which could well have constituted a basis of a sense of common identity and worldview capable of withstanding the impact of slavery. We must be sensitive to the ways in which the African worldview interacted with that of the Euro-American world into which it was carried.

Mbiti (1990) draws attention to the African worldview by discussing African indigenous religions throughout the African continent. In the traditional African ontological system, the hierarchical view of the universe with a supreme being, the Great Spirit or holy God, takes centre stage followed by lesser deities and spirits. At the core of the African worldview is the accessibility and control of the power of the Spirit or spirits in every aspect of human life. The spirits and also lesser deities possess human beings, which is expressed in people performing physical movements ritualistically. Accordingly, this ideology combines the sacred and secular or the spiritual and natural world into a holistic and harmonious system where individuals interact with each other, the supernatural and their ancestors. Community solidarity rather than excessive individualism is also an important feature of the African worldview.

Inevitably, slavery transformed the cultures of the Africans especially in the United States, which demonstrated the least degree of African retentions of all the slaves imported into the New World, certainly in comparison to those found in Caribbean islands such as Haiti. Yet, enslavement did not completely eliminate African sensibilities, albeit reconfigured under conditions of extreme brutality. In particular it is maintained that religious life in the diaspora is one of the strongest areas of African retention despite the systematic acculturation of West African slaves (Herskovits 1958). Scholarly research suggests the slaves retained some practices of their African indigenous religion and reinterpreted European Christianity in the hidden swamps and unsafe terrain of the 'invisible institution', the name given to the secret times and places where Africans worshipped God during the days of slavery (Raboteau 1978). The religiosity of the slaves was a syncretism of the Christianity given to them by their European slave masters in the new environment, a point that will be developed further in Chapter 1.

Writing of the Jamaican situation, for example, Hewitt (2016, p. 3) explains that:

> In spite of all the efforts by the religious and political apparatus of the colonial system that were geared at de-Africanising the Jamaicans of African descent their retention of the religio-cultural resources of their homeland went deeper into their sub-consciousness. Even when missionary Christianity was employed as a tool to de-culturalise Africans of their

> religious worldview, the umbilical cord with the Motherland of Africa was too strong to be broken.

I argue that aspects of the African worldview or 'Africanisms' prevalent in the Caribbean can also be discerned among black Caribbean people in Britain. The challenge in studying the retentive embers of Africanism is that African religious practices are embedded in the song, narrative and riddle tradition, and African societies tend to be skewed to orality. The ways in which the slaves translated Christianity was through the spoken word, more so as they were forbidden to read and write. The prominence of orality in Pentecostal preaching, arising from the African American context, has remained one of its most notable characteristics, and it would be useful to briefly contextualize oral literacy in Africa as a point of reference for analysing this preaching tradition.

Oral versus written literacy in preaching

Oral and written literacy are often seen as two binary poles, with orality considered the lesser of the two in spite of its bourgeoning contours. Finnegan (2012) presents a stalwart argument for oral literature to be accorded the same status as written literature, explaining that their differences are in degree rather than in kind. She rightly confirms that both oral and written literary genres are centred on words. It is also apparent that cultures have different emphasis on literacy, and the use of oral media varies at different times and geographical settings. The continued function of the oral tradition does not rely on the lack of writing nor disappear because of the transcription of oral texts. Given globalization and the rapid pace of technology the notion of an oral–literate continuum would be more befitting to describe literacy in many societies rather than ascribing a purely discrete oral literate state.

Several African societies are marked by written as well as oral literacy (Draper and Mtata 2009), pointing to an oral–literate continuum. As Zeleza (2006, p. 17) argues:

> There were African societies that were literate long before the imposition of European colonial rule. Moreover, the two, orality and literacy, do not necessary mark sequential stages; as several scholars have amply demonstrated there has always been a dialogic interaction between them.

However, in several African societies, there is a rich oral tradition manifested in the transmission of knowledge, attitudes and ideas (Okpewho 1992). Oral literature by its definition depends on a performer who formulates words for specific occasions and it is also communal.

Preaching in African Caribbean Pentecostal spaces is primarily dependent on oral literacy even when homilies depend on the written form, though it is possibly more accurate to describe contemporary preaching as reliant on an oral–written tradition. The performative and communal aspects of oral literature, inherited by Pentecostal ministers who actualize verbal literacy in preaching, are mediated through a range of linguistic components. This preaching also matches well with a traditional category of rhetoric known as epideictic, where in some definitions the main purpose of language is to showcase the orator's verbal abilities. Thus, African Caribbean Pentecostal preaching can be interpreted as an oral literary genre in its own right.

Communicating texts in preaching

It is paramount to focus on how preachers communicate texts, as preaching does not function in a cultural or linguistic space and the ethnography of speaking offered by Hymes (1972) focuses on language in the social context. He explains: 'such an approach cannot take linguistic form, a given code, or speech itself as a frame of reference. It must take as context a community, investigating its communicative habits as a whole' (p. 2). His perspective can be applied as a framework for analysing the language of preaching as a part of the African communication system (ACS) used by diasporans.

Therefore the study of preaching has two dimensions: the

linguistic which centres on areas such as lexis, phonology, syntax and semantics, and the stylistic which outlines the ways in which these different elements are combined to create a variety of effects. The two will be separated for the purposes of analysis although there are points of overlap. This book first describes the linguistic characteristics of speech in the diaspora, and second identifies the range of stylistic features found in Africa that have been retained by diasporans, particularly in Britain. It is especially in the area of stylistics where the African persistence in the diaspora remains constant, not only in sacred but also in secular domains (Tomlin 1988, 1999).

An analysis of African Caribbean preaching includes the 'text', that is the Bible, and the process of its interpretation by both preachers and congregants. Sermons reveal the exegesis of biblical texts by these Pentecostals. Generally, preaching does not merely focus on hermeneutics or written, verbal and non-verbal communication, but also on how the underlying beliefs influence the reading of biblical texts. Consequently, the process of interpretation of the Bible by African Caribbean Pentecostals should be seen in light of their inherited African worldview and oral culture, integrated with their religious practices formed out of slavery, colonialism and contemporary life in Britain.

Structure of the book

The book comprises eight chapters and falls into two main parts. Part 1 provides the historical and language background and discusses the theology of preaching. Chapter 1 summarizes the historiography of Pentecostalism and follows the retention theme by focusing on the African roots of Bishop William Joseph Seymour and the Azusa Street revival. This chapter alludes to the transportation of Pentecostalism from North America to the Caribbean, particularly Jamaica.

Chapter 2 presents the Windrush migrant population during the post-war period, as a backlight for the development of African Caribbean Pentecostal churches in Britain, and outlines the theologies of these churches. In addition, it examines the liturgical praxis including prayers and singing, music, dancing and hand clapping as a setting for the act of preaching.

Chapter 3 discusses the linguistic aspects of communication as a backdrop to the homiletic practices, artistry and style of preaching. As Jamaicans are the largest Caribbean population in Britain, the history and development of their language is the focal point for preaching in this book. The preaching event for the first generation is presented as a distinct system of communication, negotiated through the use of Jamaican Creole (JC) and Standard English (SE). It analyses the African Caribbean vernacular spoken by second and third generations by focusing on SE and the respective local varieties of English, JC and British black talk (BBT), proposed by Tomlin and Bryan (2009). Since British-born ministers tend primarily to speak SE or the local varieties, the description centres on their ability to code-switch, whereby they switch from SE or its localized variant to JC or BBT. Chapter 3 also explores the linguistic repertoires of clergy cross-generationally through a textual analysis of sermons.

Critically, Chapter 4 offers a hermeneutics of African Caribbean Pentecostal homiletics. It examines ten broad areas of homiletic praxis such as a plenary view of the Bible, interpreting biblical texts and preaching in context. The chapter draws attention to the role of theological education and approaches to sermon preparation and delivery. It also explores the impact of prosperity theology on African Caribbean preaching.

Part 2 examines the performative and stylistic facets of preaching by focusing on the communicative skills of the clergy and the range of verbal tools employed. Chapter 5 examines the artistic oratory of black Pentecostal preaching through a discourse analysis of exemplar homiletic texts characterizing components such as improvisation, creative use of language and proverbs. Additionally, non-verbal elements including the dramatic presentation of self are discussed.

Chapters 6 and 7 describe two other major stylistic devices: call and response and repetition. Chapter 6 explains call–response as being symptomatic of the ACS and a fundamental core of preaching. It describes its subdivisions, for example, encourager, overlapping and the performer's cue. The different forms of repetition, such as near repetition and lists, are considered in Chapter 7. The functions of repetition and the dramatic and crescendo effect enhancing the exposition of preaching are also featured.

Chapter 8 considers the implications of African Caribbean preaching as a prophetic voice and tool for liberation. It suggests that this genre of preaching has had a significant impact on the spiritual climate of Britain.

Prompts for reflection and activities are included at the end of some chapters and the appendices. These activities are based on the techniques and strategies utilized in African Caribbean Pentecostal preaching. They are primarily designed as a pedagogical tool for homiletic educators. Clergy across the Christian traditions are encouraged to focus on their own homiletic practices by exploring ways to engage with the excerpts of sermons that are presented. The reflection and activities should also prove invaluable in supporting sermonic preparation and delivery.

PART ONE

Backgrounds

I

Development of Modern Pentecostalism: Its Origins, African Roots and the role of William Joseph Seymour

> It is a largely ignored fact – yet one of crucial importance – that the Pentecostal movement owes its birth, at least in part to the black understanding of Christianity which developed as a syncretism of African folk belief and western Christianity in the crucible of American slavery. (MacRobert 1984, p. 3)

This chapter will consider the historiography of Pentecostalism and also examine the African roots of Pentecostalism and the Azusa Street revival in Los Angeles, considered the birthplace of modern Pentecostalism in the West. The cultural and religious heritage of Bishop William Joseph Seymour, a key figure involved in its inception, will also be the focus of attention. The passage of Pentecostalism to Jamaica will be referenced as a frame for the subsequent chapter on African Caribbean Pentecostal churches in Britain.

Origins of Pentecostalism

The precise origins of Pentecostalism lie within a biblical tradition of ecstatic spirituality that dates back to the Old Testament prophets. However, its inspiration is primarily drawn from the experiences of the Apostles who spoke in tongues, recorded in the biblical account of Acts 2. There are two types of tongues: a divinely inspired language, which is known, but which has never been studied, referred to as xenolalia, evidenced in Acts 2; the other glossolalia is a divinely given language known only by God (see Acts 8.17–19; 10.44–46; 19.1–6). Reports of glossolalia, although related to the apostolic era, have been observed throughout the centuries among Christians and non-Christians alike.

It is worth mentioning that there are challenges in defining Pentecostalism and as Yong (1999) explains, it is almost impossible to 'essentialize' it theoretically, more so as it often dovetails with Neo-Pentecostalism, the Charismatic, and Neo-Charismatic movements. Nevertheless, Anderson (2013, p. 7), citing Douglas Jacobsen, provides an adequate definition: 'In a general sense, being Pentecostal means that one is committed to a Spirit-centred, miracle-affirming, praise-orientated version of the Christian faith.' The experience of the Spirit may or may not include speaking in tongues as 'initial evidence' of baptism in the Spirit, which is fundamental for many classical Pentecostals. Anderson (2013) rightly explains that Pentecostalism has consisted of a variety of local movements with particular contextual responses to imported forms of Christianity.

The increasing attention given to the historiography of Pentecostalism as an academic study is reflected in scholarly research such as those of Robeck (2014) who cites several narratives found within almost all early Pentecostal historical sources globally. He further underscores reports of revivals and outpouring in diverse places including the following: Wales (1904–05); Khassia Hills of northern India (1905); Pandita Ramabai's mission in Mukti, India (1905–06); the Hebden Mission in Toronto (1906); the Korean Pentecost of Pyungyang, Korea (1907) and among the Methodists in Valparaiso, Chile (1909).

There are also competing narratives regarding the history of Pentecostalism in the West, though the birthplace is generally accepted as 312 Azusa Street, Los Angeles in 1906 led by William Joseph Seymour, emerging from a prayer meeting held by a largely black congregation at 214 North Bonnie Brae Street. Up until the 1970s theologians presented the narrative of Charles Fox Parham as the father of Pentecostalism or Parham and Seymour as co-founders, or Seymour as one among many originators. The multiple-centres theory of Pentecostalism points to other origins as equally important, such as William Durham's mission in Chicago and Gaston Barnabas Cashwell's mission in North Carolina. The disregard for the contribution of African Americans especially in the early writings can be partially explained by a combination of bias rooted historically in the socio-political context of a racially divided American society, and unreliable and misrepresented of primary and secondary sources. Significantly, a further reason for this 'neglect' also lies in Parham's claim that Seymour had promoted a counterfeit revival which was due to the residual element of 'truth' Seymour had received at Parham's Houston Bible School (see Espinosa 2014).

Academic research by scholars such as Nelson (1981), Hollenweger (2005) and Robeck (2006) confirm the role of Seymour as the main protagonist at Azusa Street. Espinosa's (2014) excellent study supports Seymour as the key player and challenges some recent views of the multiple-origins theory of Pentecostalism. He also contends that although Seymour and his peers were not the only ones responsible for classical global Pentecostalism, 'they were the "single" most important leaders and centre, and catalyst among many for its origins … though not its subsequent development in the United States from 1906 to 1909 and around the world' (Espinosa 2014, p. 30). Azusa Street was ultimately an interracial and multi-ethnic phenomenon created by Africans and white Americans that also contained other nationalities (Daniels 1999). Nevertheless, Seymour and his fellow worshippers in the early Pentecostal movement had an African heritage, sharing a common religious expression, which is relevant to our understanding of the early Pentecostal movement as a precursor for the elements contained in African Caribbean preaching.

The African roots of Pentecostalism and Bishop William Joseph Seymour

In order to extrapolate the African roots of modern Pentecostalism, it is imperative to highlight the orality of the slave community in the New World. The private and mainly oral tradition of slave religion means that there is limited written evidence of their liturgical practices. Drawing on an oral religious context, there were no Bible or written creeds, liturgies and hymn books to translate and conduct services. Many slaves were either illiterate or semi-illiterate and were prohibited by law to read and write, but they did not diminish the significance of biblical texts. Many preachers were able to memorize whole biblical passages, sermons or hymns they had gleaned while attending white church services. The largely African oral culture made the Scriptures accessible. Orally gifted ministers were able to weave elements from African culture or anecdotes from their captivity. These sermons were full of hope for ultimate freedom, which would be transmitted to their compatriots.

The Azusa Street revival had taken place only 40 years after the emancipation proclamation, giving slaves their freedom, which is significant as African American Christians at Azusa Street were either former slaves or the children or grandchildren of former slaves who had inherited elements of African spirituality. The African base of Pentecostalism is seen in the ways that black Christians had interpreted Christianity during the slavery era, expressed in particular through their worship style that consequently influenced the early Pentecostal movement. There is evidence that the worship patterns of black Pentecostals had profoundly influenced white Christians and other nationalities that attended the revival (MacRobert 1989). Ironically, one of the criticisms that Parham had of Seymour's endeavours, apart from Seymour's lack of 'truth', was the mission being eclipsed by the 'fanaticism' and 'fleshly' 'Negro' practices 'pawned off on people all over the world as the working of the Holy Spirit' (cited in Espinosa 2014, p. 8).

It must be noted that the Africanisms manifested in shouting, dancing, jerking, Spirit possession by 'falling out', or being 'slain in the Spirit' (signalled by falling to the floor), visions and trances, were a part of black and white revivalists' worship for decades prior to Azusa Street. Writers such as Alexander (2011) claim that many behaviours identified as African retentions were found among predominantly white congregants in the camp meetings of the nineteenth century. The worship style of the Great Awakenings, although primarily led by whites, attracted blacks because they displayed behaviours found in traditional African religion.

Echoes of African religious motifs were clearly visible in the liturgy and theological praxis at Azusa Street. The total immersion of one's self being set aside for God's use reverberated the African view of the coexistence of sacred and temporal in all aspects of life. African retentions were manifested in singing combining the hymns of their Holiness ancestors with Negro Spirituals. Throughout Africa, music, singing and dancing are also transfused in every aspect of life and enacted in spirituality (Alexander 2011). Congregants at the mission responded to the Holy Spirit by running, jumping, dancing the holy dance, similar to the ring shout of the slaves, and 'falling out', reminiscent of African ecstatic worship. They sang and spoke in known and unknown tongues and also uttered prophetic words. The moans, groans and melodies were expressed in an African style, communally with the leader of a song singing each line while the congregants joined in an antiphonal way. Individuals had trances and visions. The openness to supernatural encounters albeit through the Holy Spirit reflected another obvious African religious import. The heavy involvement of women was a notable feature of the revival and centred on biblical approval of Joel 2.28–29, and reflected African ontology. The inclusion of women in the spiritual world, serving as priestesses, for instance, is an African preservation that values the contribution of women in all aspects of the community.

It is important to mention that Seymour, the son of emancipated slaves, inherited the culture and religion of the slave community he experienced growing up in Louisiana. He and his compatriots from Azusa Street grew up in an abyss of racism. As Nelson (1981) surmises, Seymour's religious philosophy was grounded in the Bible and the invisible institution of black Christianity. Pentecost for Seymour meant not only speaking in tongues, but included a wider social view of the power and gifts of the Spirit. His faith, shaped by the world of African American Christianity, encompassed freedom, equality and community. Freedom from sin entailed allowing one's total being to be immersed by the Spirit of God. Freedom also meant being liberated from slavery and oppression. It was equality for all, including black people, and the community enmeshed with God intertwined with each other. Seymour's egalitarian views reflected his desire for multiracial fellowship and providing opportunities for ministry participation irrespective of class and gender. His theology regarding the equal standing of every person before God was reproduced in the constituents at Azusa Street comprising men, women, rich, poor and an array of ethnicities and nationalities, although the movement was later marred by racial tensions. He also believed in the heart of religion in every facet of life, including the eschatological view of the Second Coming of Christ that would balance the scales of justice, especially for black people who could not achieve this on their own. He believed in spiritual powers attained through possession by the Holy Spirit, trances, visions, dreams, prophesies, healing and exorcism. Seymour's theology and liturgy at the Azusa revival were mainly expressed through an oral narrative reflective of the post-slavery community.

Robeck (2006, pp. 117–19) suggests that Seymour's preaching style, based on verbatim recordings of an oral presentation rather than a written sermon, represented two characteristics found in African American preaching. The first is the reading of one or two quotes from the Bible at intervals, a common method for some African American preachers to work their way through the text. It is evident in a short excerpt of a sermon by Seymour entitled: 'The Holy Ghost and the Bride'.

> We read in Revelation 22.17. 'The Spirit and the bride say come.'
>
> Oh how sweet it is for us to have this blessed privilege of being a co-worker with the Holy Ghost. He inspires us with

> faith in God's word and endues us with power for service for the Master. *Bless His dear name*!
>
> Every man and woman that receives the baptism of the Holy Ghost is the bride of Christ. They have a missionary spirit for saving souls. They have the spirit of Pentecost. *Glory to God!*
>
> *'And let him that heareth say, come; and let him that is athirst, come; and whosever will, let him take the water of life freely.'*
>
> Oh what a blessed text. The bride of Christ is calling the thirsty to come to Jesus because this is the work of the Holy Ghost in the believer. He intercedes for the lost; He groans for them.
>
> The Spirit also calls the believer to come to Jesus and get sanctified. He points the sanctified to Jesus for his baptism with the Holy Ghost. When you are baptized with the Holy Ghost, you will have power to call sinners to Jesus, and they will be saved and sanctified, and baptized with the Holy Ghost and fire. *Amen!*

In this excerpt we can see the quotation from Revelation 22.17 in the first part and from Revelation 22.17 in the second. Seymour's reflections follow each part of the quotation.

Other excerpts illustrate a second practice, common to black Pentecostal clergy that Seymour applies. Preaching as a dialogue with the congregation is undergirded by call and response wherein the preacher makes a statement or a comment, presents an image, or recounts a story and the congregation responds by talking back to the preacher (call–response will be discussed in Chapter 6). Throughout the years call–response has characterized Pentecostal preaching in many parts of the world. It is highly probable that call–response found its way from the African American practice.

Clearly, an African American minister led the Azusa revival, and African American members influenced the style of worship enormously. However, as Robeck (2006, p. 138) argues: 'It would be unfair to claim that the only influence that played a role at the mission was the African American one – non-African

Americans did bring their own gifts and experiences.' At the revivalist camp meetings of the previous century both whites and blacks contributed to the mission's music, preaching and prayers. Some of the radical worship services in various Wesleyan holiness congregations in Los Angeles had given scope for white people to also shout or to be 'slain in the Spirit'. The diversity of people such as African Americans, Latinos, Armenians, Russians, Swedes, Germans, Japanese and Chinese converged on the mission at Los Angeles and found expression in their worship.

Racial and doctrinal issues

The multiracial nature of the early movement was one of its most positive features (Daniels 1999), but it was later tarnished by racial tensions, with detractors such as Parham who fired an arsenal of racial attacks on the worship style and against Seymour. Outside critics fuelled by secular newspapers also disparaged the worship at Azusa Street, comparing it to pagan rites. Consequently, separate black and white Pentecostal churches developed by 1914 as racist attitudes reflecting Jim Crow America resurfaced and became entrenched.

Apart from racial issues, doctrinal disputes erupted at the mission. Seymour and the first Pentecostals subscribed to a Wesleyan holiness view of sanctification, believing in a 'second work of grace' following conversion, but added baptism of the Holy Spirit, evidenced by speaking in tongues, thus making the Christian experience a three-stage process. Whereas William Durham's fierce promulgation of his two-stage proposal, the 'finished work of Calvary' included sanctification complete at conversion and the believers' maturity in holiness as they grew in grace. This doctrinal debate divided the movement and resulted in the formation of the white-dominated two-stage Assemblies of God in 1914. These two-stage Pentecostals rejected the Wesleyan holiness view of sanctification and reinterpreted Durham's teaching of sanctification as a continuous process rather than the immediate removal of sin at conversion.

Additionally, there was some opposition to the Trinitarian doctrine that emphasized the tripartite nature of God, the view of the vast majority within Pentecostalism. Oneness groups emerged who critiqued the classic Christian doctrine of the Trinity as polytheistic, and their advocates claimed that monotheism required the existence of only one God, not three persons in one as espoused by the doctrine of the Trinity. The Oneness or 'Jesus Only' Pentecostals spearheaded by Canadian evangelists Robert McAlister and John Scheppe thought of Jesus as the name of God and required their adherents to be baptized, or as in the case of Trinitarians to be re-baptized, in the name of Jesus following the formula used by the Apostles in the book of Acts. The new controversy permanently divided the movement into two theological groups.

Pentecostalism in Jamaica

In spite of the racial and doctrinal divisions within Pentecostalism, both black and white American Pentecostals from the Trinitarian and Oneness traditions have been instrumental in spreading the tenets of their faith to various part of the world, including the Caribbean. Significantly, Pentecostalism had landed on the shores of Jamaica by 1910 but did not make a huge impact until after the Second World War when it became the fastest growing religious movement. The religious landscape of Jamaica up until that time saw historic denominations in the form of Anglican churches and other spiritual expressions such as Myal, Cumina, Revival Zion and Pocomania that bring together elements of African and European religious traditions. The rise of Pentecostalism was accompanied by the decline of groups such as Cumina, etc. In general, white American missionaries in Jamaica were instrumental in its initial development, but its rapid growth from the early 1950s was in the main due to the leadership of indigenous ministers, who became Pentecostals while working in the United States. When these ministers returned to Jamaica they established indigenized Pentecostal churches, which combined the status of Christian denominations with the revivalists and indigenous cults. Morrish (1982) gives an insightful account of the syncretistic cults in Jamaica, postulating that the African–European roots of these cults were even more evident than the bicultural origins of American slave religions. Pentecostalism, because of its syncretistic nature, was particularly amenable to indigenization. MacRobert (1990, p. 2) says:

> The Pentecostalism of the black American, William J. Seymour – which had been 'de-Africanised' by white Pentecostals – was reinvigorated with the leitmotive of black folk belief and black dignity. The themes of freedom, equality, community, heaven-sent revolution and spiritual power accompanied by possession, trances, dreams, prophesying, healing and exorcism were mediated through the oral narrative liturgy and theology of the syncretistic sects and cults ... was reaffirmed in indigenised Jamaican Pentecostalism.

The history of Pentecostalism in America and its importation especially to Jamaica has been critical in tracing its development among African Caribbean people in Britain.

Summary

Attention has been given to the origins of modern Pentecostalism by focusing on its African roots. The historiography of Pentecostalism had claimed Charles Fox Parham as the initiator. Further research by some historical revisionists record the leading role of William Seymour at the Azusa Street revival in Los Angeles, considered the birthplace of global Pentecostalism. Of equal significance are the African elements found in the worship patterns of the revival, but influences from other cultural groups also had an impact on the style of worship. Despite the challenges of early Pentecostalism, both racial and doctrinal, the movement spread and reached Caribbean islands such as Jamaica. One of the reasons for its remarkable growth in Jamaica after the Second World War lay in the appeal of its combining aspects of Jamaican 'folk beliefs' grounded in the African religious system and Western Christianity.

2

African Caribbean Pentecostalism in Britain: Theologies, Liturgy and the Preaching Event

In the previous chapter we explored the history of Pentecostalism in North America and its African roots as a backdrop to its extension in the Caribbean, particularly Jamaica. Pentecostalism from Jamaica to Britain can be traced to the mass migration of the Caribbean population during the post-war period. This chapter will examine the development of African Caribbean Pentecostalism established by the early migrants commonly referred to as the Windrush generation, and provide a summary of the theologies of black Caribbean churches. It will also draw attention to the gender composition of preachers and discuss the liturgy and worship template in these Pentecostal spaces. In addition to the principal structure of worship, the chapter will outline prayers intertwined with music, singing, dancing and hand clapping as a milieu for the preaching event.

The charting of Pentecostalism from Jamaica to Britain does not operate in a historical vacuum. Peter Fryer's seminal text, *Staying Power* (1984) and the writings of Walvin (2001) demonstrate that the history of African people in Britain is extensive. Olusoga's (2016) brilliant and evocative research, popularized in the BBC television series *Black and British*, attests to people of African descent having a long history in the British Isles dating back to the third century AD. Although black people have been in Britain throughout the centuries, the post-war period marked the beginning of mass migration of people from the Caribbean on the MV *Empire Windrush* in 1948, to fill the labour gap. The early migrants came from islands that had historic links with Britain such as Jamaica, Barbados and Montserrat. The number of migrants in 1954 was 10,000 which quadrupled in 1955 to 42,000, then becoming stable for the next two years.

The 1960s saw the enactment of progressively more stringent legislation on immigration and by the 1970s, mass immigration had virtually come to a halt following the 1971 Immigration Act, which put severe restrictions on family reunification and chain migration. Estimates of the Caribbean population provided by the Office for National Statistics latest census of 2011 suggests that there are over 600,000 black Caribbean people (approximately 10 per cent) of the total British population, then, of 61.4 million.

The development of African Caribbean Pentecostalism in Britain

The existence of Summer Road Chapel is recognized as the first black Pentecostal church, established in 1906 by Thomas Kwow Brem-Wilson, but it was not until the Windrush generation that a plethora of African Caribbean churches were established. Two of the largest church organizations, New Testament Church of God started by the Jamaican pastor, Oliver Lyseight, and the Church of God of Prophecy, initiated by the English minister, Herbert England, were first established in the 1950s.

As a major religious movement African Caribbean Pentecostalism was previously under-researched. Hill (1963) and Calley (1965) were among the earliest writers. The insightful studies of MacRobert (1989), Gerloff (1992) and Toulis (1997) in some ways signalled a turning point in the area for successive black Pentecostal theologians from the 1990s onwards. Scholars such as Edwards (1992), Beckford (2000), Aldred (2005), Sturge (2005) and Adedibu (2012) provide an illuminating overview of the history, theology and 'distinctiveness' of African Caribbean Pentecostal churches. Edited works by Aldred and Ogbo (2010) and Thompson (2013) outline various leadership issues associated with the political and socio-economic challenges facing these churches in the twenty-first century.

The reasons for the emergence of African Caribbean Pentecostal churches in Britain in the 1950s are multifaceted. The Windrush generation came from Pentecostal denominations in the Caribbean, which they re-established in Britain partly because of a desire to continue practising their faith within their denominational affiliations and identities (Aldred 2005). Many individuals perceived white churches as being spiritually cold and dead and preferred Caribbean worship styles (Tomlin, 1988, 1999). This was not only the view of migrants who were in the Pentecostal tradition, but also of those from the established churches (see Wilkinson 1993), some of whom defected to Pentecostalism. In fact, according to Adedibu (2012, p. 103) the burgeoning of African Caribbean churches in Britain was the consequence of 'transferred growth from the historical denominations, as most of the West Indian migrants who pioneered West Indian churches in Britain during the Windrush era were from historic churches'. In addition, it has been argued that 'black' Christianity (Pentecostalism) is socially, culturally and theologically different from 'white' British Christianity (MacRobert 1989). Cross-cultural misunderstanding may also have played a role, with the reserve displayed by some British people interpreted by the newcomers as hostility. There were cross-generational considerations as well. Most migrants in the 1950s were young whereas the congregations in white inner city churches were often elderly. Despite these factors, some early Caribbean Christians, such as Oliver Lyseight, the first national leader of New Testament Church of God, received a warm reception and preached in both mainline and Pentecostal churches. While some Caribbean Christians had positive experiences, covert racism was practised in some local white churches (see Brooks 1982 for instance) though much of it was unintentional. Anecdotal evidence drawn from Caribbean migrants suggests that some of them felt excluded by their fellow white Christians and in a few cases were even politely instructed not to return to churches occupied by the host community. Incidentally, my mother recounts having such an experience. The early migrants had a mixed reception in white sacred spaces, but it is also apparent that African Caribbean churches developed as a buffer from the harsh realities of British life. It may be argued that these churches still serve this function.

In fact, the Race Disparity Audit (2017), for instance, paints a complex but vivid picture of how African Caribbean people are treated across public services. The wider social, political and economic factors inextricably link to the continuation of these Pentecostal churches. In response to societal exclusion, proponents of black theology from British Caribbean theologians such as Beckford and Reddie, drawing on the writings of James Cone (1970), for instance, view the church as a vehicle for liberating people from oppressive systems. Liberating theological models remain a contested area among African Caribbean Pentecostals but its relevance for preaching shall be explored through Beckford's bewitchment hypothesis in Chapter 8.

Theologies of African Caribbean Pentecostalism

At the risk of merely essentializing the theologies of African Caribbean Pentecostalism, we will attempt to focus on five main strands. First, the Church of God movement that started from a revival among poor whites in North Carolina towards the end of the nineteenth century, which became Pentecostal under the influence of Azusa Street, and was indigenized in the Caribbean (Gerloff 2000, p. 95). Second, the Oneness or Apostolic movement found in the urban ghettos of the United States which travelled to the rural areas of Jamaica, before coming to Britain. Churches such as Bethel United Church of Jesus Christ and Pentecostal Assemblies of the World are included in the Oneness tradition. Gerloff classifies the third group as Healing Pentecostals (known also as the Word of Faith movement) who are strong advocates of miracles, influenced by American Healing Evangelists such as A. A. Allen, R. W. Schambach, Morris Cerullo and Kenneth Copeland. The fourth group identified by Aldred (2005) emerged from the 1990s onwards. These are independent churches started by second-generation British-born ministers such as Bishop John Francis who founded and leads the largest of these churches, Ruach City Church, with an estimated membership of 6,000. A fifth theological tradition has developed within the twenty-first century based on the 'Five-Fold' ministry model identified in Ephesians 4.11–13 including apostle, prophet, evangelist, pastor and teacher. Churches such as Restoration Fellowship Ministries in Birmingham and Qadosh Kingdom Movement based in Ilford, Essex, are in this category. Its proponents emphasize the restoration of the apostolic–prophetic ministry and are headed by an apostle. African Caribbean churches that pattern the Five-Fold model are not directly related to Restorationists or the Third Wave movement of North America, evidencing supernatural signs. Rather their origins lie in the Caribbean Pentecostal movement that demonstrates the miraculous and like Restorationists desire to return to a form of Christianity based on the apostolic era.

In spite of the differences in the theological traditions of African Caribbean Pentecostal churches, there are overarching theological hallmarks, succinctly outlined by Beckford (2000). They emphasize 'salvation' and are concerned with 'radical transformation', resulting in fire and brimstone themes of repentance in their message, and being driven by the Spirit. According to Beckford (p. 6) 'the black church in Britain can be understood as a family'. As he goes on to explain, black churches were established by groups of families and kinship networks were employed to recruit new members. These churches uphold and preach about values that sustain and nurture families. Additionally, the church is a family in the wider sense of the word as each member is considered to be a brother or sister. Obviously, all Christians irrespective of ethnicity see themselves as belonging to the family of God. However, this notion may possibly have a stronger resonance for African Caribbean Pentecostals because as a social group they are marginalized in mainstream society and to some extent, the mainline or historic church.

Men, women and preaching

It is worth mentioning that in these Pentecostal churches the gender leadership is typically male. Finding support from the Apostle Paul's controversial texts regarding the role of women in church services, for example, 1 Timothy 2.11–15, male leadership reflects the ecclesiastic domain globally. One notable exception is the Jamaican-led Pentecostal City Mission where six of the presiding bishops are women and three are men. Alexander's research (1996) had indicated that there were more African Caribbean female Pentecostal ministers than in most mainline British churches. Recent years have witnessed an upsurge in the numbers of black female clergy, with some married women ordained as co-pastors leading collaboratively with their husbands, and an increase in single women becoming assistant or senior pastors. An explanation for the emergence of female preachers in these Pentecostal churches could be the predominance of women, many of whom are single, linking also to anecdotal evidence surrounding the lack of men coming forward for ordination. Another contributory factor could be the complex gendered relationships in these churches. While men hold visible authority, women wield a tremendous amount of influence, understood as 'silent collusion' in the relationship dynamics of Caribbean men and women (see Foster 1991). Therefore, within this Pentecostal context, it has been possible for a few women to dislodge the patriarchal hegemony but invariably they are accountable to higher-ranking male ministers. Given that there are female preachers among African Caribbean Pentecostals, this book includes preaching exemplars from both genders as a collective and an analysis of women's preaching vis-à-vis men will not be undertaken in this work due to the relatively small numbers of female Pentecostal clergy and the fact that preaching is primarily carried out by men despite the progress of women in ministry (Gilkes 2001). Having said that, it is recognized that women impart spiritual knowledge in several other ways apart from the pulpit, through music, prayer, literature, etc., and the women's agency within these churches transcends the sphere of formal ordination (Butler 2007).

The sermon, also known as 'the word' or 'the message', is the highlight of the service. A member of the ministerial team which within this context comprises, bishop, pastor, elder, deacon/deaconess, missionary, evangelist or minister often presents 'the word'. A minister in this sense is someone who is gifted in ministry but does not have the equivalent rank of an ordained pastor or elder, and their name is prefixed with the title minister when they are being addressed, for example, Minister Abigail. First-generation preachers in particular are referenced by their surname, for example, Pastor Caine. In the Caribbean and North America this practice has continued but within Britain this is not the case among the younger generation, who tend to address each other on a first-name basis even if they use the prefix pastor, deacon and so on. As some churches embrace the five-fold ministry model, an apostle and a prophet/prophetess are often included in the ministry team. Laypersons gifted in oration are sometimes given opportunities to 'preach the word', and the criteria for preaching are sometimes based on spiritual maturity and biblical knowledge. Laypersons may also give exhortations that are short sermons presented by one or two individuals, especially during special services such as a youth or women's convention/convocation.

Liturgy

There are striking similarities in the liturgy and worship style of African Caribbean Pentecostal churches whether or not they subscribes to a Trinitarian, Oneness or Five-Fold theological persuasion. Like their forerunners at Azusa Street, they do not typically have a written liturgy but as Sturge (2005) rightly explains, there are predictable worship patterns that regular congregants can identify. Increasingly, some churches incorporate a written order of service, possibly attributed to the higher levels of literacy among the second and third generations compared to their forebears. Nevertheless, there is a great deal of latitude within a 'predictable format' and an expectation from congregants that services should be 'led by the Holy Spirit'. These sacred spaces are characterized by some extemporization within a very well defined and rigid template, not always apparent to the outsider.

The context in which most speech events take place in these Pentecostal churches is fixed and associated with specific structures, not only in Britain, but also throughout Africa and the diaspora. The principal speech events within the main Sunday worship service are prayers, Bible reading, singing and preaching. There are also 'testimonies', which usually form a part of the Sunday evening service. Other special services such as all-night prayer meetings are held periodically. So too are conventions or convocations, but increasingly in some churches, seminars and conferences centred on a particular theme such as finance or gendered relationships are included, and are replacing the more traditional convention-type services.

An overview of a model Sunday morning worship service is given below, based on a summary of the descriptions provided by Edwards (1992) and Sturge (2005), my own previous research (see Tomlin, 1988, 1999) and findings from current observations. A worship leader, also known as a moderator, is responsible for leading the service, and usually begins with a prayer, followed by a 'devotional', consisting of singing, Scripture reading and further prayers. A time is set aside for giving financially, known as tithes and offering; a tithe is approximately 10 per cent of one's income and church members are expected to 'pay tithes'. A choir and/or praise and worship team usually sings during the tithes/offering segment of the service accompanied by congregational singing, clapping and dancing. Worshippers sing and dance while they place their tithes and offering into the basket, or ushers are assigned to collect the monetary gifts, row by row. Notices are given, sometimes followed by special singing, which can range from a soloist to the choir or praise and worship team and is often regarded as the prelude to the preaching event. The climax of the service is the sermon or 'the word'/'the message'. The success of the entire service is often dependent on the quality of the sermon. Invariably an 'altar call' is made after the message whereby those who are not 'saved' or committed/born-again Christians are invited to join the faith by standing or kneeling in front of the altar. (An altar is not necessarily a physical object but the space at the front of the podium or lectern). Christians are also often encouraged to 'come to the altar' to pray for any situation affecting their lives.

Prayers

It is worthwhile to discuss specifically the role of prayers as each segment of the service is undergirded with prayer, either individually or congregationally. Individual prayer occurs when one person prays aloud while the congregation listen. Whoever is praying individually is given tremendous support by congregants with loud verbal responses including 'amen', 'hallelujah', 'yes Lord', 'thank you Jesus', and what can be described as intoned guttural sounds such as 'hmmmh', an African retention. In more traditional churches it is not unusual for two or three individuals to pray concurrently, though this practice in Britain is becoming obsolete. The term 'traditional' in this sense is used to describe churches that have a significant amount of Caribbean influence in liturgy, preaching language, etc. Churches such as Triumphant Church of God seem to fit this category. Praying concurrently is distinguished from congregational prayer, which involves everyone praying aloud at the same time. During the time of the 'devotional', prayers might be individual or congregational. If a particular worship service is deemed to be at a lull, congregants are directed by the moderator to pray to enliven or lift the atmosphere. It is believed there are demonic forces that can hinder the smooth running order of the service and that these evil elements can be expelled through the power of prayer. An individual or congregants collectively pray for the minister or layperson just before he or she delivers the sermon or homily. In addition, whoever is presenting the sermon often prays for themselves. The clergy, and sometimes those who are 'altar workers' involved in the prayer ministry team, often pray for those who are ill or 'going through', a phrase meaning to experience unfortunate circumstances and challenges. Sometimes congregants sing very softly or hum a tune of a song fairly quietly when an individual is praying. Often background music accompanies prayer. In fact, all services have an extremely high degree of singing and music, dancing and hand clapping which are clearly an African import and, as MacRobert (2003) posits, music and rhythm connect individuals to the Spirit, expressing spiritual possession and power. These elements also feature in the preaching event.

Singing and music, dancing and hand clapping

In her research Dixon (2014) describes how the early migrants transported congregational singing and music, key aspects of African Caribbean Pentecostalism, based on the worship traditions of the singing of Euro-British hymns, Euro-American gospel hymns, and 'old-time' (Jamaican) choruses. The singing of Euro-British and Euro-American hymns and 'old time' choruses are still retained to some extent but dependent on the generational composition of the church. Dixon critiques the gross absence of systematic and historical research on the genesis of black gospel music in African Caribbean Pentecostalism, which she argues tended to be heavily slanted to the African American version of gospel music that framed a universal 'one-size-fits-all' paradigm. According to Dixon (p. 7), 'Now in the 21st century, the style of religious singing and music that emerged out of the congregational worship experience of black Pentecostalism during the post-war years in Britain is recognized as black gospel music.' It would appear that contemporary gospel singing and music in British Caribbean Pentecostalism seem to have several influences such as reggae and the African American gospel genre and is also being affected by African singing styles, seen in the songs of popular Nigerian gospel artists such as Sinach. Contemporary Christian songs composed by white British artists, for example, Tim Hughes, and Australians such as Planet Shakers and Hillsong are also influencing gospel music in Britain. Hillsong, in particular, as a global Christian music phenomenon is played in these churches but as Pauline Muir (2017) asserts, the sounds, tones and melodies are 'blackenized'.

Singing and music play a pivotal role in preaching. Ministers often sing before or after a sermon and sometimes sing a short verse of a well-known song in the middle of their presentation to affirm a point they are explaining. An analysis of the liturgy of some of the popular gospel songs from Africa, the Caribbean, North America and Britain reveal their underlying theology as a basis for the sermon. For example, the belief in God's providence in seemingly impossible situations can be demonstrated in the following songs in varied geographical settings: 'Making a Way Out of No Way' by Bishop John Francis (Britain); 'He'll Make a Way' by Travis Greene (North America) and 'Waymaker' by Sinach (Nigeria). Note the use of the word 'way' to denote God's omnipotence. The keyboard is also played at certain points during the sermon, which is possibly borrowed from the African American context. The playing of the keyboard complements the lyrical delivery and unique tonal presentation of some preachers, demonstrating African retentions, as tonal inflections characterize several West African languages.

Dancing and praise break

Dancing in traditional Western churches has by and large remained absent, although the Great Awakening brought a resurgence of dance in worship continuing to the modern era. We saw in Chapter 1 that dancing was also an important part of worship for early Pentecostals, demonstrating African persistence in the style of dancing. In Jamaica, dancing for Pentecostals and religious groups such as Pocomanians is a fundamental aspect of worship (Taylor 2001). In Britain, dancing is also characteristic of African Caribbean Pentecostalism. In some churches there is also a special kind of dance known as 'praise break'.

The praise break entails a break from a segment of the service including the sermon, where congregants engage in exuberant worship by dancing or shuffling their feet with extreme rapidity or by jumping up and down while moving their arms or clapping their hands in unison. Reminiscent of the ring shouts of the Caribbean and American slaves, this phenomenon has filtered into African Caribbean churches in Britain. The young people at Lee New Testament Church of God, Quadosh Kingdom Movement and Ruach City Church engage in a praise break. Bishop John Francis from Ruach often employs a praise break at certain points during his sermonic discourse. A praise break is usually accompanied by an improvised musical ensemble, especially the keyboard.

Hand clapping

Hand clapping is another form of worship generally. Oosthuizen (1979) observes that in traditional African societies, hand clapping is used as an invocation of the divine presence and to approach ancestors. In these communities, hand clapping often takes place not only when people dance but when they remain standing in one place. It also expresses joy. Hand clapping is a marked feature of African Caribbean churches. In the Bethel United Church there is highly stylized hand clapping lasting for several minutes. In addition, hand clapping takes place during key moments in the sermon to demonstrate when the preacher has made a point that resonates with congregants.

Responses to the Holy Spirit through sound and motion

Writing in general about the worship service in these Pentecostal churches, Sutcliffe and Tomlin (1986, p. 26) say:

> The spiritual ecstasy of black churches is striking, almost tangible, destined to leave an indelible impression on the visitor ... There is the overall intensity of the sound and motion, and the spiritual intensity associated with this. Inextricably linked with these is the mystical experience, the touch of members by the Holy Ghost.

A key element of the primal religions of Africa is the experience of being filled with the power of the spiritual. In the same way

Caribbean Pentecostals exercise and release deep emotional feelings as a response to the power of the Holy Spirit, which are manifested in many culturally distinct patterns of behaviour referred to as 'getting in the Spirit' or 'being in the Spirit'. It is often expressed in sudden jerks (seen especially among older members), and distinctive arm and leg movements. Individuals shout 'hallelujah', 'amen', 'glory' or 'Jesus', typically with hands upraised. They may also cry, dance, jump, walk or run around the church. To dance in the Spirit, to sing in the Spirit, to move in the Spirit and to speak in tongues (glossolalia) are all viewed as responses to the power of the Holy Spirit. Spirit possession occurs when the music reaches its highest pitch and singing and dancing are at its most intense. Individuals can become completely abandoned in the vortex of the moment as energy is released in a seemingly untiring manner.

The pitch of spiritual experience during a church service is reached, however, via a collective act of worship involving much emotionally charged interaction and a striking and expressive use of sound and motion. This atmospheric sound and motion can also be seen in preaching where the clergy respond to the synergy of the congregants, which intensifies and empowers the delivery of their sermons. Such use of sound is characteristic of the oral tradition of several African communities and found in other contexts in the diaspora and is not solely confined to the sacred realm. As early as 1929, Martha Warren Beckwith aptly stated that Jamaicans give expression to their inner life through sound and motion (Sutcliffe and Tomlin 1986). These phenomena are prevalent in African Caribbean Pentecostalism and are distinguishing features of the preaching act.

Summary

Chapter 1 examined the African base of Pentecostalism. This chapter analysed the development of African Caribbean Pentecostalism in Britain emerging from the Windrush generation. The theologies of African Caribbean Pentecostal churches are diverse, denoting five main strands: the Church of God movement; the Oneness tradition; churches influenced by

Healing evangelists; independent churches, and finally those based on the Five-Fold ministry model headed by an apostle. The overarching hallmark of these churches depicts human transformation within a familial paradigm. The clergy are predominantly male, but there has been an increase in the number of females in recent years. Female participation transcends formal ordination and they are active in imparting spiritual knowledge in other ways, such as through literature. The preaching event is pivotal to worship services. This chapter has provided a detailed description of the liturgical practices and components of services by discussing key elements of prayers, singing, music, dancing and hand clapping as a context for preaching. The spiritual atmosphere of these Pentecostal spaces often reflects a great deal of sound and motion, making the worship and presentation of sermons a unique experience.

3

The Genesis and Development of Jamaican Creole: Speaking Jamaican, British Black Talk and Code-switching in Preaching

The aim of this chapter is to explore the structural features of language used by African Caribbean Pentecostals. Apart from Standard English (SE) and its local varieties, three major areas of their linguistic repertoires are highlighted, including Jamaican Creole (JC), British black talk (BBT) and code-switching. A discussion on any preaching discourse has to first consider the *linguistics*, examining areas such as lexis, phonology, syntax and semantics.

Furthermore, as many of the Windrush generation or early migrants primarily came from Jamaica and significant numbers tend to be Pentecostals, the language of this group will be the context for the discussion. Jamaican migrants, as we saw in Chapter 2, also developed two of the largest African Caribbean Pentecostal churches in Britain: New Testament Church of God and Church of God of Prophecy. Critically, the first generation laid some of the foundation of preaching for the second generation. Therefore, it is fundamental at this point to explore the history and development of the language used by many of the Jamaican population in Britain.

The language of the Windrush generation: origins and development of Jamaican Creole (JC)

The Windrush generation or early Jamaican migrants came to Britain speaking JC. Recognized by linguists as a language, JC is popularly referred to as Patois, pronounced 'Patwa'. Creoles, such as Jamaican, can be found throughout the Caribbean, Britain, America and elsewhere. There are also French-based Caribbean creoles spoken in Britain by people from St Lucia and Dominica. However, the genesis of JC is the subject of much scholarly debate (Bailey 1966; Todd 1978; Romaine 1988). Part of the wider discussion on the development of JC fits into the broader issue of the origins of creoles in general, as creoles from different parts of the world share similar language features.

Development of JC

It appears that JC developed in the seventeenth century during the transatlantic slave period out of the contact situation between British slave owners and West African slaves. When the Africans were transported to the New World, as discussed in the Introduction, new languages developed from this oppressive and brutal system that became the dominant mode of communication for the people in the Caribbean. The precise origins of JC remain a bone of contention and the beginnings of creole languages in general remain unknown. Early explanations suggested that JC in common with other creoles could be traced back to a fifteenth-century Portuguese pidgin used along the African coast and later carried to Asia. Spoken by slaves who crossed the Atlantic as Dutch, French, Spanish and British cargo, this language was relexified, meaning its grammar was retained but its lexicon changed, according to the language of the European slave master. From this point of view, a pidgin arose and was able to accommodate all the languages of the European slave owner during the process of original contact. It is argued that this accounts for the commonality across New World creoles. However, the nature of that contact positing a monogenetic theory of origin for all creoles has been contested by scholars such as Holm (1988) to include a more polygenetic explanation, highlighting the occurrence of creoles in diverse spaces at different times but under similar circumstances, thus producing parallel outcomes. Most writers favour the polygenetic hypothesis but debates abound as to the exact mechanism that led to the presentation of these languages.

Bickerton (1981) for example, in line with Chomsky's universal principles of child language acquisition, attempted to explain the origins of creoles in terms of innate language formation or human biogram for language. Bickerton's Language Bioprogram hypothesis is mainly based on a comparison of evidence from creole grammars and studies of child acquisition. He postulates that the incorrect language structures characterizing children's language acquisition are similar to those manifested in creole grammars. The features children learn naturally are the ones that the children of first-generation creole speakers would have learned in the absence of direct input from the speech of others in the community. Bickerton provides a theory of first-language acquisition in unique circumstances and an explanation for the origins of creole, but his claims are highly contentious. A counter to Bickerton's views is that language acquisition is a creative and ongoing process, and it would appear that children do not create their own language but rather follow one that is already in existence which they reproduce and transform (Romaine 1988, p. 275).

The African substratum theory is of particular importance for the discussion of the development of creole in Jamaica and the African diaspora in general. From this point of view, languages such as JC are seen as having the grammatical structure of the languages of initial contact between the British and Africans. Alleyne (1980), acknowledged as the main proponent of this theory, draws attention to transmissions and continuities of African languages. He maintains that consideration should be given to significant factors of power dynamics and the language contact and interactions between European slave owners and African slaves, starting in the forts of West Africa through the Middle Passage to the plantations of the

New World. Thus, Jamaican Creole has evolved out of contact between British slave owners and a remnant of West African languages, particularly Twi, one of the many languages brought to Jamaica, but the only one which managed to survive some of the processes of language demise and extinction. Le Page and De Camp (1960) lend support for the cultural and linguistic pre-eminence of Twi in the development of JC.

It must be pointed out as a precursor for the development of the language that the unequal system of the plantation society was marked by upper and middle class whites comprising planters and other professionals such as doctors; lower class whites such as artisans; the Jewish colony; free people of colour and slaves at the bottom of the pyramid. The slaves as the oppressed group were forced to learn the dominant language, while surrendering some of their own language structures and features. The African slaves borrowed the language from all the British groups living on the islands including English, Scottish and Welsh dialects. The dominant language used by whites changed little but altered dramatically when used by slaves using the normal processes of second-language acquisition. In other words, JC is the consequence of two main phenomena: borrowings from English by African language users, and the dramatic changes in English when acquired by Africans. In a further collaborative work, Alleyne et al. (2004) explore the place of extra-linguistic factors such as political economy in creole origin. Political economy is defined in this sense as the relations of social and economic production, played out between the African slaves and their European slave masters. It centres on the ways in which work was organized for production and profit, and the interplay of the cultural reproduction in language, culture and religion, utilized to sustain the system of slavery.

As noted earlier, the grammatical structures of JC reveal retentions from West African languages such as Twi. Scholars point to the continuities of the African languages in JC, particularly Twi, one of the many languages of the slave community (Alleyne 1980, 1989; Roberts 2007). The continuities are reflected in aspects of the language such as phonology (sound), lexicon (words), and syntax (arrangement of words grammatically). Bryan (2010, p. 6) explains:

> in respect to phonology, there is possible retention of Twi sound patterns in the remnants of tone, where the contrast in pitch can change the meaning of an utterance: *it kyaang iit* 'it can be eaten/it can't be eaten'. The contrast relies heavily on pitch – the feature most clearly distinguishing Jamaican Creole from English in the way this particular meaning would be conveyed.

The evidence for African retention in syntax is apparent in the way verbs are used where two or more verbs share the same subject without being joined by a conjunction such as 'and', or complementizer, for instance 'to', as in the sentence 'carry go bring come' (Bryan 2010, p. 6). There is the use of the particle 'dem' to show a plural word, for example, 'the pickney dem' [the children]; this is similar to the Twi use of 'nom' in oyere/oyere nom for 'wife/wives'. African lexicon is present in Akan words such as 'jukka' meaning 'to pierce' (Bryan, p. 6).

Whichever view is taken regarding the origins and development of creoles in general and JC in particular, it remains open to debate and conclusions can only be tentative. This is due mainly to the lack of concrete empirical evidence centred on the history of actual spoken texts. While the history of JC is somewhat elusive, it remains the 'popular' language of Jamaica with SE as the official language (Pollard 2003).

Structure of JC

Despite issues surrounding the development of JC, it has already been demonstrated that its grammatical structure can be distinguished from SE in a number of ways. Craig (2006), drawing on the work of Bailey (1966), drew on some of those distinctions. For example, JC uses the unmarked verb, as previously indicated, with consequently no requirement for agreement with respect to number; there is no subject–verb agreement in creole. For example, 'di uman fall/di uman dem fall' (The woman falls/The women fall). As we've said, Jamaican Creole demonstrates plurality in an interesting way – it is marked with the particle 'dem', for instance, 'the bway dem' (the boys). The tense system uses the unmarked verbs as well as a particle indicating the 'past'. For instance, 'Him (b) en iit/Him did iit' (He has eaten) or (He ate). Him can also refer to her, and there is no specific marker identification for gender. Similarly, adjectives in sentences are not dependent on the joining of special verbs known as copulas or linking words such as 'is'. For example, 'de weather terrible' (the weather *is* terrible). Very often the sense of a complete sentence is determined by the context in conjunction with the specific grammatical rules of JC.

The development of JC continues to be the focus of considerable study by creole linguists. Research indicates that the language has been influenced by the speech patterns of Rastafarians (Pollard 1994) and by American English (Christie 2003). A particularly prominent feature of language use in Jamaica is the extent of variation. One often-used characterization of the language situation in Jamaica has been the description of the environment as a continuum with Standard Jamaican English (acrolect) at one end and features furthest removed from SE (basilect) at the other, with the mesolect or intermediate level in between (Winford 1993).

Attitudes towards JC

There is a long history of negative attitudes towards the use of JC, which has to be seen within the wider debate of attitudes towards the language of low status groups in general. The deficit hypothesis labelling speech that deviates from the standard as 'careless', 'slovenly' and 'lazy' has been challenged convincingly several decades ago by Labov (1973), on the grounds that languages or dialects that differ from the standard are merely different and they are not deficient in any way. Unfortunately, Caribbean creoles have a legacy of low status and much of the contention surrounds the influences of creole on education (Carrington and Borely 1977; Christie 2001; Tyson 2013).

Interestingly, the early Jamaican migrants to Britain had a deficit perspective of their language, viewing it as a sign of illiteracy (Edwards 1979). The second generation were told not to 'chat bad' and JC was labelled as 'broken' and 'bad English'. Jamaican parents understandably wanted their offspring to succeed academically and professionally, unhampered by JC influences. However, these parents failed to realize that language shapes identity and, despite their vociferous objections, many second-generation children spoke in their mother tongue with friends at home, in the playgrounds of schools, and in their Pentecostal churches which will be discussed further in this chapter. The language was in many ways a form of resistance (Edwards 1986).

In Jamaica, there has been a marked shift in attitudes towards the use of Creole, reflected in the socio-economic and cultural changes in the country that began with independence, the Black Power movement of the 1970s, the cultural dominance of Rastafarian ideology and the development of a Jamaican middle class with JC as the mother tongue (Bryan, 2001). Much of this development has been captured in the media and analysed by scholars such as Shields (2002) showing how the voice of the 'folk' and the vernacular have gained prominence. Theoretically, it has been named in the literature as 'nation language' by Brathwaite (1984) and popularized in dance hall culture (Cooper 2004), referred to as 'bashment'. The launch of the *Di Jamiekan Nyuu Testiment* (The Jamaican New Testament) in 2012 also demonstrates the wide acceptance of the language, although there are still dissenting voices on both sides of the Atlantic (Johnston 2011).

The Jamaican language in Britain

While it is apparent that JC is a fully functioning language spoken by the masses in Jamaica, the extent of it in Britain remains unknown. Clearly, the Windrush generation spoke JC and those who are still alive, such as my mother, continue to speak JC fluently. Commenting on the language of the first generation, Tomlin and Bryan (2009) suggest, based on anecdotal evidence, that many Caribbean individuals could not understand the respective dialects and accents spoken in Britain. Interestingly, Wells (1973) reports that Jamaican adults living in London adapted their pronunciation to the local variety.

To date, no empirical study nationally has been undertaken concerning the numbers of second or indeed third/fourth generation black British Caribbean individuals who speak JC on a fairly regular basis. Research in the 1980s and 1990s indicated that the linguistic repertoire of British-born people was complex. In London, Rosen and Burgess (1980) first named JC's interaction with other languages and the local variety London Jamaican (LJ). Sebba (1993) proposed that LJ was used as a marker of identity. Edwards (1986) provided evidence for code-switching behaviour in her data. From a linguistic point of view, code-switching can be defined as the use of more than one language in a single communicative act (Heller 1988) and is widespread in multilingual communities. To broaden and identify the scope of the language used throughout the country, Sutcliffe (1992) referred to the language of young African Caribbean people in London, the West Midlands and elsewhere as British Jamaican Creole (BJC), drawing attention to the degree to which it diverged from rural Jamaican speech. Sutcliffe's research suggested that the second generation used BJC, their respective local dialects and/or SE. Jamaican Creole is the focus of attention in the British literature as Jamaicans, as previously stated, are the largest Caribbean population in Britain, and the British variety of the language appears to be the most commonly spoken, not only among young black people of Jamaican heritage, but among other Caribbean and African groups, and in varied forms by young people across the ethnic spectrum (Rampton 1995). Linguists such as Sebba (2007) have described the language used by black British people as black British English (BBE). Kerswill and Sebba (2011) have called the language used by a range of ethnic groups including African Caribbean young people in inner London as 'Multicultural London English', popularized in the media as Jafaikan (fake Jamaican) and satirized by Ali G (Sacha Baron Cohen). In the case of language in inner London, Kerswill and Sebba have focused on the hybridity of Jamaican Creole, 'African Englishes', Indian English and a range of inter-language varieties, spoken alongside London English.

In the absence of data describing the national picture, I will discuss the current language situation by first examining JC usage, especially in the sacred context. This position is based on my own research in this area (Tomlin 1988, 1999, 2014) combined with ongoing participant observations as a methodology, and knowledge as a member of the African Caribbean speech community using community nomination as an analytical tool. An important trend in research is the idea of community nomination where an insider's perspective is implemented in the analysis to explore the views of the community from within (see Foster 1991).

As previously mentioned, the early Jamaican migrants to Britain primarily came from the rural parts of Jamaica. The basilect features of JC, the variation at the higher end of the creole continuum, furthest removed from SE, tended to be more widespread in rural areas (Bailey 1966). Therefore, it is highly probable that the speech of the first generation would have been extremely creolized, but their linguistic and cultural identities in many ways were tangled reflecting a post-slavery and post-colonial heritage (Mocombe and Tomlin, 2013) including negative attitudes towards JC, labelled as 'talking bad' and seen as a marker of illiteracy or lack of intelligence (see Sutcliffe 1982). In spite of these attitudes the first generation have still retained much of the basilect features of JC, particularly when communicating on a social or casual basis with each other. Clearly, the first-generation migrants are aware of JC and SE as two distinct language codes. Consequently, within formal contexts as in the sacred space, many of them continue to make strenuous attempts to speak SE, often resulting in a great deal of hyper-correction (see Pollard 2003) and affectation, referred to in JC parlance as 'speaky-spokey'. For example, 'We tank God that he has spare our life anoder day'. Some of the common words that are pronounced incorrectly include the following:

Mortgage – morgrege
Certificate – cer-fi-ti-cate
Crisps – crips
Aluminium – aluminum
Film – flim

Often, the speech of the first generation would be the hub of humour for the second generation, many of whom mimicked the communication patterns of their elders.

JC and code-switching in preaching

Many of the first-generation preachers were gifted orators and as they became settled in British society they developed their ability to code-switch. This inference is based on the premise that they were surrounded by British English, including the received pronunciation (RP) of the BBC radio and television presenters of the time, together with the respective local accents and dialects as they tended to be concentrated in deprived white inner-city areas (see Mocombe and Tomlin 2013). However, the transfer of JC features was still evident in the presentation of their sermons. Take the following example from a first-generation minister, Pastor Peterking:

Pastor Peterking	You see all dem bway dat a pley music (Can you seen those young men playing musical instruments?) You see all dem? (Can you see all of them?) If they don't stay with God, God help dem (If they do not continue on the path with God, God help them.)

As previously stated, in JC the particle 'dem' is used to show the plurality of boys as in the case above 'dem bway'. The word dem also denotes the word them; the sense in which this word is used in this instance is similar to several creole words in that it depends very much on the context of the sentence.

Pastor Peterking used the term 'all dem' to signify more than one individual. If he made reference to one boy, he would have used the definite article 'the' but pronounced it as 'de'. In addition, the word 'bway' here refers to young men but it could also mean a young boy.

The basilect features of JC were also replicated by some of the second-generation British-born people (Edwards 1979, 1986). When the young second-generation Pentecostals in the 1960s and 1970s spoke JC, despite being reprimanded for doing so, they would invariably utilize some of the basilect features (Edwards 1979, 1986) for this was the language spoken among adults in both the home and the church (Tomlin 1999). The black Caribbean Pentecostal church today is possibly the main space where JC is spoken in its variable forms. Second-generation churchgoing individuals in particular were raised, and are still surrounded, by first-generation creole speakers, but some are not able to speak JC fluently for sustained periods of time and there is significant code-switching and mixing. Take the sermon delivered by Revd Jackie Reid entitled 'Walking In the Glory of the Lord' where we can see evidence for code-switching behaviour from English to JC:

> To walk means to be in motion, to move; it is a physical activity. When we are walking we are moving. We are going in a particular direction; we are going towards a goal. We use the term walking in the physical sense to perform a physical activity; it can also be used in the metaphorical sense, meaning to stand for something like when the Bible says in Amos 3.3 'two cannot walk unless they agree', or as me mudder would sey, you better min how you wark an nek sure you wark good. (As my mother would say you had better be careful about how you walk) [conduct yourself] and ensure that you 'walk good' [so that your character is not brought into disrepute].

Take the following by another second-generation preacher, Bishop John Francis from Ruach City Church:

Bishop John Francis	You don't sit down there and fret all night.
Congregational response	Amen. Yes. Hallelujah.
Bishop John Francis	You don't sit down and cry all night.
Congregational response	Glory, amen, praise the Lord.

Note the creole influence in the phrase 'you don't sit down there and fret all night'. The phrase 'sit down' is not to be taken literally and in JC such phrases are used metaphorically. Since some of the lexicon or vocabulary is dependent on the old English of the seventeenth century, words such as fret meaning to worry or anxiety, are still a part of JC and used by the second generation. From a theological view Jesus in Matthew 6.34 implores us not to worry, a similar theme taken up by the Apostle Paul in Philippians 4.6. Therefore, congregants are aware of these key biblical texts. The call and response element of this extract will be dealt with in Chapter 6.

Take another example from the bishop where he rebukes some of the congregants about their ill-mannered behaviour:

Some of you are just rude
You rude, you rude, rude, rude
Some of you have no manners ...

The repetition of the word rude is typical of JC usage where very often points are made forcefully by the stylistic device of repetition. A more in-depth analysis of repetition will be outlined in Chapter 7.

The second generation, including preachers, are able to speak JC, especially in the West Midlands area in places such as Birmingham, Wolverhampton and Dudley, which have a significantly high churchgoing Jamaican population. Many of the second generation who speak JC do so only at key points in their sermons, mainly to convey a strong message, to add humour and to enliven a homily dealing with a theologically dry subject matter. For instance, one minister invariably says, 'excuse mi patwa' when explaining concepts which relate to theological principles or when quoting his parents, as in the following examples:

Some of you too puaan puaan in yu faith
(Some of you are too weak and wishy washy in your faith.)

My mother sey 'if you wan good you nose hafi run' (Jamaican proverb)
(If you want to be successful then you have to work extremely hard.)

Jamaican proverbs, in particular, are used frequently in sermons, and will be discussed in greater depth in Chapter 5. Proverbs are highly valued in JC and are used by both the first and second generations.

Factors for JC usage among second-generation preachers

The use of JC among second-generation preachers, particularly in conurbations such as Birmingham is possibly due to five main factors, the first being the predominance of Jamaicans in certain geographical areas such as the West Midlands (see Edwards 1986). I have travelled extensively throughout the UK for the past 35 years and can report that second generation people in these localities seem to be more fluent speakers of JC, compared to those in other parts of the country. My mother, who visited Birmingham in the early 1970s, was alarmed at the number of young children, apparently born in Britain, who as she termed it 'talk bad'. The Jamaican culture is pervasive in cities such as Birmingham, evidenced also in the use of the basilect features of JC.

A second plausible explanation for JC usage among the second generation is that during the 1960s and 1970s British-born individuals interacted socially in school and elsewhere with Jamaican-born children who arrived in Britain during that period. This was certainly my experience and I vividly recall many children in Leeds, my home town, coming from either Jamaica or St Kitts/Nevis (in Leeds, the predominant Caribbean population is Kittitian). Families invariably comprised children born either in Jamaica, some other Caribbean island or Britain. British-born siblings obviously interacted with their Jamaican-born counterparts and there would have been what can be described as language exchange and interchange between Jamaican and British-born children. Admittedly, given the lower status of JC, there would have been greater pressure for JC-speaking children to conform to the British speech patterns of their British-born siblings; however, based on my field research for an ESRC (Economic and Social Research Council) funded study based in the West Midlands, some of the British-born children became more fluent in speaking JC (Edwards 1986). Another interesting phenomenon is that some children who were born in Britain were sent to Jamaica and returned to Britain as teenagers or young adults. Therefore, it is not difficult to see how JC in Britain could be both facilitated and maintained.

A third reason also linked to the amelioration of JC can be located to the spread of Rastafarianism, and the stylized discourse patterns of Rastafarian speech, which had a huge impact on African Caribbean young people in the late 1970s and early 1980s (Pryce 1979). The Rastafarian movement originating in the 1930s has to be seen against the ideology of black consciousness and the Pan-African movement of Marcus Garvey, and the backdrop of colonial Jamaica leading to some of the rural poor rejecting British rule and identifying instead with the Ethiopian monarch, Haile Selassie or Ras Tafari. Many of the second generation were attracted to the 'dread'/Rastafarian movement or at least influenced by 'dread' – even those who converted to Christianity. As a young person, I engaged in 'reasoning' sessions, part of the Rastafarian language culture, involving the creative presentation of JC. The attraction of an alternative lifestyle and values affirming what is understood as 'black culture' for the second generation, disillusioned with the treatment they received in Britain, should not be underestimated, and although Rastafarianism has declined in popularity, it has had a long-lasting effect on black British Caribbean culture. A crucial aspect of the 'Rasta' identity involved speaking a form of JC known as 'dread talk', and the 'I-n-I' signature posturing gained tremendous momentum among African Caribbean men in particular (Jah Bones 1986).

The fourth possible explanation is that both first- and second-generation men appear to use more JC forms in their speech compared to women, and men tend not to modify their language. Research suggests that speech modification is more typical of women than men and this could be centred on the lower status of women in general compared to men (Xia 2013). Xia also confirms that women tend to pay more attention to the use of the target standard language compared with men, which she attributes to the need for women to aspire to those deemed 'better' because of their subordinate position in society. Connor et al. (2004) report that African Caribbean women have the highest participation rates in higher education, which could further explain this anomaly. Mocombe, Tomlin and Showunmi (2016) find evidence for black females in Pentecostal churches on both sides of the Atlantic academically outperforming their male counterparts. The early Caribbean female migrants worked as nurses/auxiliaries for the NHS (Dodgson 1986) and possibly felt that they had to adapt their speech accordingly, whereas the men were confined to the manufacturing industry (Mocombe and Tomlin 2013). Most second-generation preachers are men, which could account for the manifestation of JC in preaching, but the majority of congregants are women.

Finally, the upsurge in travel to Jamaica among the second generation in recent years, primarily to visit relatives, has also aided in the continuation of JC. It is not uncommon for words, popular secular songs and antiphonal choruses from Pentecostal churches, in vogue in Jamaica, to be transported to the shores of the UK. Take for instance, the chorus: 'A fi mi Jesus too' (it is my Jesus too) and the sermon entitled 'Man a Dust' (Human beings are Mere Dust) both of which became well known in Britain among African Caribbean Pentecostals. In addition, there are several thousand Jamaicans who have settled in Britain during the last 20 years or so, despite stringent immigration laws. In my own church in Birmingham, for example, approximately 40 per cent of the congregants have come from Jamaica within the last 20 years and are first-language JC speakers.

In addition, it is worth noting that JC usage by second-generation African Caribbean people comes from a variety of other sources including reggae/ragga and the dancehall music genre of Jamaica. Tomlin and Bryan (2009) propose that the language spoken by the second and third generation is a hybrid of the respective local dialect, SE, interspersed with BJC or more precisely JC words with vestiges of the phonology of African American English. Moreover, the Americanized speech from the African American Hip Hop culture (Mocombe, Tomlin and Callender 2016), gospel artists and black and white preachers who frequently visit Britain have significantly affected the speech patterns of black British people (Tomlin 1999; Tomlin and Bryan 2009). There are second-generation preachers who have adopted a slight American accent in their preaching.

Black British talk (BBT)

Tomlin and Bryan (2009) call the hybridity of language or dialect used by many black Caribbean people in Britain, black British talk (BBT). Interestingly, BBT is spoken to some extent by the second and especially third generation, whether or not their parents or grandparents come from the Caribbean or from Africa. Preachers will sometimes code-switch from SE or the local variety to JC and BBT. Take the example of Pastor Nathan Turner from the Rock New Testament Church:

> 'I haven't got time' (stated in the local Birmingham accent)
> 'to chat about ya ...'
> (The term 'chat' is a JC term for talk and 'ya' is BBT for you.)

Among the younger generation of preachers in particular there is often an interplay of language use between the respective local varieties of SE to BBT. In spite of the lack of in-depth empirical data of the language situation of young people, most casual listeners of black British interlocutors are able to distinguish between these speakers and those from other ethnic groups; however, this is not always the case, as previously alluded to, in large urban areas such as London or Birmingham where some people irrespective of their ethnic background utilize aspects of JC speech patterns. While some African Caribbean speakers may not employ distinctive JC structures in their speech, using the respective local variety or accent, most individuals utilize in their communication the stylistic features of JC that are a part of African communication system (ACS), such as repetition and dramatic presentation of self. It is this performative aspect of the language that has been most retained throughout the generations (Sebba 2007).

Class and language in sacred space

The performative nature of African Caribbean speech is significant, and on the surface it may appear that many interlocutors utilize British local dialects and their language features approximate more white British English than JC. Nevertheless, many of the current generation speak in a distinctive way which they describe as 'slang' (Tomlin and Bryan 2009). I have observed that some of these individuals are able to code-switch between the local accent/dialect or SE and a deep form of 'slang' using words which are unintelligible to the outsider. Outsider in this sense does not necessarily refer to ethnicity, for there are young people from a wide variety of ethnicities who socially interact with those of an African Caribbean heritage, hence it is used here to mean generationally. It can be argued that the political, social and economic exclusion of many black Caribbean people from several mainstream institutions contributes to the development of their own linguistic repertoire. Trudgill's (1990) work helps to explain how accents and dialects are interwoven in the fabric of British society and are markers of social class and thereby inclusion or exclusion. It is not clear whether accents and dialects are linked in the same way for African Caribbean middle class people. Recent research suggests that there is an emerging black middle class in Britain (Rollock et al. 2015). Evidence suggests that African Caribbean people with a church background are academically achieving (Channer 1995) and anecdotal reference suggest that the churchgoing British-born population are perceived as middle class.

Researchers are giving increasing attention to the tensions in the conception of black Caribbean middle classness (Mocombe, Tomlin and Wright 2014). One writer who presents an insightful description is Archer (2009, p. 6) highlighting the:

> struggle between dominant discourses that conflate authentic (and 'cool'/popular) blackness with working classness as both imposed by dominant white society and as articulated from within minority ethnic collectives and participants' resistance to 'pretentious' versions of ME [minority ethnic] middle class identity.

The authentic 'black' middle class in Archer's study were often constructed as 'out there' but 'not for me'. This rejection was used to distance the self from the *perceived* negative aspect of white middle classness such as pretence, snobbery, including the markers evidenced in the historical elites as opposed to the socially mobile and as a strategy for managing the challenging identity conflict experienced by respondents. Archer's findings corroborate the study of black Caribbean middle class families by Rollock et al. (2015). In exploring the self-identity of class, some participants self-identified as working or middle class but the majority were hesitant and ambivalent about occupying a dual identity that is both black and middle class. Mocombe and Tomlin (2013) maintain that constructs of identities within racialized societies, such as Britain, present challenges for many African Caribbean individuals born in Britain where ideas of middle classness and professionalism are synonymous with being white, while poverty, the street life and BBT are seen as the representation of so-called 'blackness'. Unfortunately, research does not report on the patterns of speech among black Caribbean middle class/professionals. However, I have observed on numerous occasions second-generation educated preachers who utilize the performative aspects of BBT. If, as research suggests, many African Caribbean people, especially women, have acquired education as mature adults (Connor et al. 2004), then it could be theorized that the second generation may still lack, in Bourdieu's frame, the cultural and linguistic capital to fully participate in British society; they may not be attuned to certain nuances or the subtle forms of SE due to their position in British social strata based both on their class and ethnicity, thereby implicating the reproduction of their language in social spaces such as the church. The use of BBT may solidify the so-called 'black' identity of African Caribbean Pentecostals, particularly in the sacred context where the biblical notion of unity is enmeshed in the web of cultural/ethnic identity.

Summary

Attention has been drawn to the development and linguistic structure of JC, as the language spoken by Jamaicans who are the largest Caribbean population in Britain. It was theorized that the Windrush generation primarily came from the rural parts of Jamaica where the basilect features, the furthest removed from SE, were most prominent in their speech. The first-generation preachers utilized JC and were surrounded by local varieties of English, SE and RP leading at times to hypercorrection. The maintenance of JC among the second generation is dependent on a number of plausible factors such as Jamaican-born individuals interacting with their British-born siblings and the influence of Rastafarian ideology and its concomitant 'dread talk'. JC usage appears to be more widespread in cities such as Birmingham with a large Jamaican population. The language of second-generation African Caribbean people is multifaceted though there is a lack of empirical data. Second-generation British-born preachers use SE/local varieties and code-switch to JC, especially in humour or to reprimand. The language situation among second and third generations has also been discussed with reference to Tomlin and Bryan's BBT. The language of preaching has been analysed in terms of the complex nature of the language context and in relation to gender and class.

4

The Hermeneutics of African Caribbean Homiletics

This chapter will explore the meeting points of African Caribbean homiletics through hermeneutical lenses, and will identify the distinct characteristics of African Caribbean Pentecostal homiletics and its shared features with global Pentecostalism. It will first draw attention to the theological and educational background of the clergy.

The early migrant Caribbean preachers were largely uneducated and untrained in homiletics and they tended to present sermons from memory and extemporarily without the aid of written notes. The Bible as the 'written word' was very often the only source to which reference was made. Individuals with the ability to preach could be 'called upon' without prior notice to 'deliver/bring the word' and the view was that one should be ready to 'bring the word' at any time, presumably based on the Apostle Paul's invocation to Timothy to 'Preach the word! Be ready in season *and* out of season' (2 Timothy 4.2). This practice is virtually outdated in Britain, particularly with the younger generation, many of whom are increasingly becoming educated theologically through attending courses at institutions of higher education such as Queen's Foundation, Birmingham and the Universities of Birmingham and Roehampton. Some aspiring ministers have also attended institutions in North America that link to their denomination such as the Church of God's Lee University in Cleveland, Tennessee; while others have attended Bible schools or courses established by their own local denomination or church. A case in point is Ruach City Church who have developed their Certificate in Practical

Theology. Despite these promising trends there still remains a paucity of rigorous theological education.

Muir (2015) suggests that the reason for the lack of theological training among Pentecostals in general is historical and equally applicable to blacks and whites, as they often share similar concerns regarding theological education. He explains that in the formative years of the Pentecostal movement there was reluctance to 'privilege education'. Indeed, in many quarters there was outright antipathy and animosity towards the emergence of liberal theology from the nineteenth century that questioned the inerrancy of Scripture, the God of miracles, and the dynamic power for missions evidenced in Spirit baptism. For Pentecostals who maintain a fundamental view of Scripture, this resulted in a 'dead church'; powerless to reach the 'unsaved' and spiritually ill-equipped for the 'end time' mission to usher in the Kingdom. Muir (2015) also believes that this challenge continues to the present day in Pentecostal/Charismatic practice. This issue has implications for the hermeneutics of Pentecostal preaching, which will be discussed with reference to African Caribbean homiletics below.

African Caribbean Pentecostal homiletics

The shared framework in the liturgy of African Caribbean Pentecostalism, discussed in Chapter 2, provides a platform for its convergence in preaching. As previously stated, the preaching event is the most prominent feature of African Caribbean Pentecostal ecclesiology, and one which also plays a pivotal role in Pentecostalism generally. Inevitably, African Caribbean preaching mirrors aspects of global Pentecostalism but there are distinct characteristics. It must be stressed that any attempt to posit a matrix of preaching has to consider its multifarious nature, for preaching is also dependent upon individual personalities and proclivities, which diverge from mere reductionist analyses. However, we will outline African Caribbean Pentecostal homiletics, especially contemporarily, by focusing on the following ten broad areas:

1 Expressive and performative nature of preaching
2 Deductive versus inductive sermons
3 Approaches to sermonic preparation and delivery
4 Pentecostal hermeneutics and theological education
5 Plenary view of the Bible and interpreting biblical texts
6 Preaching in context
7 Preaching against worldliness
8 Attire as signifiers
9 Life situation and serial preaching
10 Influence of prosperity theology.

1 Expressive and performative nature of preaching

The premier homiletician Fred Craddock makes the important point that both content and method of preaching are pertinent to theology. This is useful to bear in mind when analysing any type of homiletic model including those in the Pentecostal tradition. Focusing on the early Pentecostals, MacRobert (1989, 2003) states that Christianity was expressed in narrative theology, the shout, the song, the dance, distinctive African motor behaviours accompanied by polyrhythmic clapping of hands, stamping of feet and swaying of bodies. He further explains that such worship is found among Jamaican Pentecostals and replicates the patterns found in West Africa. In black Pentecostal preaching in general there is a high display of expressive behaviours and a 'certain license of freedom in the preaching moment' (LaRue 2011, p. 890). Interestingly, MacRobert's earlier work centred on the British context, drawing attention to the degree of culturally expressive behaviours dependent on the denominational affiliation. African Caribbean churches under the leadership of white Pentecostals in North America (for example, New Testament Church of God) appear to be more restrained compared with Oneness groups headed by African Americans where there is no pressure to conform to the norms and expectations of white Pentecostals.

Equally, while cultural manifestations are demonstrated cross-generationally some of the second and third generation seem at times to be more reserved in their worship compared with their forebears, but this still depends to some extent on the type of church they attend. This variance may also be attributed in part to the hybridity of their culture which can be considered as a fusion of aspects of British and Caribbean. However, the expressive behaviours described by MacRobert are prevalent in preaching and can be seen cross-generationally, irrespective of the denominational affiliation. Ministers who are highly rated seem to be those who are outstanding communicators with the ability to utilize distinctive African communicative styles such as call–response and repetition discussed in depth in Chapters 6 and 7.

Preachers who communicate biblical texts are expected to bring 'the word' to life and in this sense the preaching can be seen as performative. Writers such as Thomas (2016) explain the performative nature of sermons. The preacher is expected to embody the word of God including head or rationally, heart or emotionally, and body or physically. The word is embodied and brought to life or incarnated in the total being of the preacher and not solely confined to the rational part of his or her being, hence the preaching act can accurately be described as performative.

2 Deductive versus inductive sermons

In terms of both its exegetical undergirding and sermonic structure, deductive preaching has been established as normative practice. Based on the Enlightenment rationalistic hermeneutical paradigm, this homiletic mode seeks to filter biblical texts into propositions irrespective of their original form or genre. Meanings of texts are conveyed to listeners in a linear fashion and sermons progress sequentially with clear argumentation, concluding with specific applications for the listening audience, a seemingly monologic sermon style, which affirms the authoritarian role of the preacher, disconnected from the audience. Commenting on Craddock's work, Cosgrove and Edgerton (2007) state that he recognized that the traditional deductive three-point sermon was rapidly losing ground in the early 1970s and that this led to his new method.

Craddock's New Homiletic proposal of the 'inductive model' engages listeners from passive recipients into active participants. This heightens the listeners' role in the preaching event and transfers the making of meaning of the text from solely the preacher to that of the listener. In this way the preaching event becomes dialogic, unlike (as he sees it) the flat, lacklustre and passive listening of deductive sermons, diverging from the old traditional and kerygmatic preaching of Karl Barth.

LaRue (2011) contends that Craddock's concerns regarding the deductive three-point sermons are justifiable but primarily addressed to white preachers in mainline churches and that in the black church the deductive three-point sermon did not have the same negative impact as it had on some white congregations. Even though LaRue writes about African American sermons, his ideas are equally applicable to African Caribbean Pentecostals. As LaRue (2011, pp. 497ff.) states:

> The idea of a boring preacher or an overly authoritarian preacher thundering broadsides to a disconnected, discontent audience is not what the three-point sermon wrought in the best of black preaching. Not then, not now. The three-point sermon in the black church is clothed in imagination, humour, playful engagement, running narrative, picturesque speech, and audible participation on the part of the congregation.

LaRue advocates that the three-point sermon is not the issue, but that it is the *boring* three-point sermon that must be rejected. He rightly affirms that black preachers must be exposed to other methods of preaching.

Jiménez (2015) argues that the deductive style often found in Pentecostal preaching in the Caribbean is a relic of colonialism with its stress on individualism and authoritarianism, that during the colonial times invested certain individuals with authoritative powers which maintained the social order – including slavery. He calls for the deductive preaching style to be deconstructed, aimed at liberating people, and that there must be a critical dialogue with the New American Homiletic school.

3 Approaches to sermonic preparation and delivery

It is important to return to the theme of orality, discussed in the Introduction, to underscore the act of Pentecostal preaching among African Caribbean clergy, as it is critical to spiritual formation, consigning significance to orality. Hollenweger (1992) asserts that Pentecostal theology emerged out of the African American oral context and it can be argued that the early Pentecostals' emphasis on orality has continued globally well into the twenty-first century. As Alexander (2011, p. 43) states:

> This orality held important implications for the development and spread of Pentecostalism, which for most of its own history has been conceived of as largely an oral tradition. Even today the global Pentecostal movement has seen its greatest growth within cultures that incorporate an oral communication mode.

Martin (2015) confirms the critical role that preaching played in the Pentecostal movement and opines that Pentecostalism's oral nature may have been diluted to some degree in the West as a consequence of education, but confirms that preaching still remains a dominant aspect of Pentecostalism. The inherently oral nature of Pentecostal preaching is sometimes viewed as a somewhat distant relative to the more formal homiletic practice found in historic churches, and is conspicuous by its absence in mainstream literature. This is similar also to the perceived superiority of written over oral literacy. It must be stressed that all sermonic approaches are equally valid and there is much to learn from differing approaches.

A popular method for sermon preparation and delivery in mainline denominations such as the Anglican tradition is to preach by way of a lectionary, where there is a predetermined structured cycle of the liturgical year with associated Scripture readings which starts on Advent Sunday, at the end of November or beginning of December. The cycle of readings takes place over a three-year period and there are typically four types of readings from the Bible. The first is taken from the Old Testament, the second is usually a psalm, the third from the New Testament and the final reading comes from one of the four Gospels. The sermon is usually the theme for that Sunday or an explanation of the reading is provided. The lectionary is invaluable in helping ministers prepare sermons and provides a basis from which they can work. Many lectionary preachers tend to execute their sermons in a thematic way, drawing from the texts, the Christian year and the particular time and circumstances of their congregation's life. In contrast, a thematic approach for Pentecostals does not rely on a structured cyclical year, time, etc., as they do not subscribe to a lectionary approach. According to Thomas (2014), whose findings are from his research of the homiletic practices of 12 black Pentecostal churches in the south London area, the lectionary can serve as a hermeneutical framework to provide a more systematic approach to preaching.

Lectionary preachers believe in the role of the Holy Spirit reflecting the ideals of Christianity globally, but sermons tend to be tied to the liturgical year. However, African Caribbean clergy maintain that the Holy Spirit should be at liberty to completely change the direction of the sermon including the topic or theme and the actual content, which sometimes happens minutes before the actual delivery of a sermon. I have observed some excellent sermons that were unprepared beforehand. On the one hand, as Thomas (2014) asserts the Holy Spirit should be present in sermon preparation and one should not have to wait until mounting the pulpit to gain inspiration, but on the other, he contends that the lectionary preachers should be conscious of the Holy Spirit's role to change the direction of the sermon or topic, if necessary, and the lectionary should not be strictly adhered to when mounting the pulpit to deliver the homily. Clearly, there is much to glean from each method of sermon presentation.

A common approach to preaching in general is the expository method, deriving from the Latin word 'setting forth' or 'making accessible', where the content and theme of the homily progresses in a linear way. The aim of this kind of sermon is to illuminate faithfully a message from Scripture by making it accessible to contemporary hearers. There are two central principles in expository preaching. The first is that the authority of Scripture in the pulpit is paramount. In other words, the preacher's message must authenticate the Scripture. The preacher or expositor attempts to understand the biblical text on its own merit, apart from personal inclination or doctrinal principles. The second relates to the clarity of the preacher's message in that it should be clearly expressed in language using simple logic, comprehensible to everyone.

There are two principal types of expository preaching: verse-by-verse exposition and thematic exposition. In verse-by-verse expository preaching, the preacher selects a passage and divides it into smaller consumable units of thought, and then proceeds with an exposition of each verse in a systematic manner. The exposition of each verse reflects a coherent biblical theme or spiritual truth through the interrelationship and application of ideas. In thematic expository preaching, the preacher draws on the sermon theme from the biblical text, but reveals that theme in whatever mode seems relevant to making the message coherent to congregants. It is distinguishable from verse-by-verse exposition in that the expositor moves in and out of the biblical text in a way that is not necessarily verse-by-verse (Newton 2016). It would appear that the preaching most revered by white British Pentecostals historically and presently tends to be expository with a sequential exegetical approach (Kay 2015).

In general, a basic approach to preaching is the developmental one where the sermon contains one central idea or main aim that is worked out through a series of a few progressive stages where the idea or purpose reaches its climax. In contrast, the homiletic approach of the first-generation Caribbean Pentecostals does not follow this modus operandi, but is extemporaneous and without notes, as briefly mentioned at the beginning of this chapter. It is also episodic. According to Graves (2006), the episodic approach to preaching is based on a series of vignettes stitched together like a quilt. David Buttrick's seminal book, *Homiletics* informs current thinking on episodic preaching. Rather than viewing the sermon as consisting of an introduction and three points, Buttrick conceives the sermon as a sequence of moves which combine to communicate an idea or evoke a response in the listening audience. He articulates that there should be no more than six different topics in sequence. The sermons of the Windrush generation are episodic both in terms of Buttrick's conception and the actual style of preaching. In some cases there are several 'moves' that appear at times to be unrelated. Links between topics tend to be marked by intonation and coherent strategies connecting points are not always explicitly stated. This type of organizing principle in verbal texts represents an African construct and as Draper and Mtata (2009, p. 1) eloquently state, 'The collective representation of oral tradition in performance is what constitutes African religious worldviews, which are usually implicit and assumed to be known rather than explicitly stated.'

Implicit themes are inferred from a series of concrete anecdotes. This episodic style of preaching, a departure from the linear homiletic model, has led to criticisms by some of the second generation that the content and exposition of sermons by the first generation are unstructured, and lacking in thematic clarity. The second and third generations still retain an episodic approach to a great extent but due to enhanced education and theological training it is combined with a more developmental method. A few individuals preach from memory and without notes, while many depend or at least utilize notes as an aide-memoire. Within this framework of preaching there is a great deal of improvisation or spontaneity, which will be explored in depth in Chapter 5.

It is useful to mention that contemporary preachers will sometimes encourage congregants to take notes if they are explaining certain theological concepts such as justification. Both young and middle-aged congregants sometimes make notes based on the sermon. This is indicative of a more literary approach to biblical learning, which was not undertaken by the first generation, many of whom had basic literary skills, and therefore relied on memory to engage with sermonic texts.

Alternatively, note-taking is conducted when congregants consider the sermonic discourse to be more didactic, which they are able to gauge from the presentation of the homily.

Within the African Caribbean preaching genre, there is a significant amount of sound and motion, previously explained in Chapter 2, where spiritual energy is released in a synergy of movement between the minister and congregants. Preachers who demonstrate a high level of intensity in their discourse, often marked by this synergy, are viewed as more 'anointed' or spiritual. Congregants base sermonic satisfaction on the delivery of the text engaging the African communication framework as well as the content of the actual homily. Sometimes there is insufficient theological engagement through study and an over-reliance on the enabling 'power' of the Holy Spirit. Pentecostals may well heed the often quoted advice of the Apostle Paul in 2 Timothy 2.15 (KJV) 'study to shew thyself approved unto God, a workman that needeth not to be ashamed, rightly dividing the word of truth.' Nevertheless, for Pentecostal preachers the Divine (the Holy Spirit) hermeneutics must mediate insights of Scripture.

4 Pentecostal hermeneutics and theological education

The primacy of the Bible is the cornerstone for the Christian faith, and ecclesiastic leadership would concur with Long's (2016) definition that normative biblical preaching should be where the Bible is the major text. In Pentecostalism, the interpretation of the text is coupled with supernatural and experiential spirituality. The belief in the supernatural reflects the underlying hermeneutics of Pentecostal homiletics and the supernatural phenomenon of speaking in tongues in Acts 2 is not merely seen as a historical account. In the African Caribbean faith community, the supernatural is unconsciously translated through the lens of the African worldview, with a tendency to see spirituality in every aspect of life. For Caribbean Pentecostals, spiritual battles and the demonic realm are very real, given credence by the popular biblical verse, 'For we wrestle not against flesh and blood, but against principalities, against powers, against the rulers of the darkness of this world, against spiritual wickedness in high places' (Ephesians 6.12, KJV). The battle between righteousness and evil is seen as a constant one. While Pentecostals in general berate the 'wiles' or 'schemes' of the devil, in African Caribbean Pentecostalism evil can also be seen in 'obeah' (Jamaican term for witchcraft) and individuals being 'set upon' through the medium of obeah or witchcraft, seen as an integral fabric of the spirit world practised by a few non-Christians. The belief in satanic conflict and the Christian's ability to be 'victorious' in conquering demonic onslaught is revealed in some of the 'old time' choruses and even contemporary songs. Take the following choruses:

> Move satan move, let me pass, move satan move let me pass
> Move satan move, let me pass
> For I am born again
> I'm saved and sanctified.
> Move satan move let me pass.
> (Jamaican chorus)

> In the name of Jesus, in the name of Jesus we have the victory. In the name of Jesus in the name of Jesus satan will have to flee, tell me who can stand before us when we go in Jesus' name, Jesus, Jesus precious Jesus we have the victory.
> (origins unknown)

Regarding doctrine, Pentecostals globally tend to focus on historical books rather than didactic works, often seen in their preference for the books of Luke and Acts. Pentecostal preachers tend to read the New Testament through Lukan eyes, especially through the lens focused on Acts. One of the reasons for the overemphasis on the Luke/Acts frame among Pentecostals, including African Caribbean, could be due to the missionary character of the Pentecostal movement from its beginning, following Jesus' charge in Mark 16:15 to preach the gospel to everyone.

Throughout the varied Christian denominations, the tools to

interpret and clearly present scriptural truths by clergy are seen as keys for enhancing the spiritual depth of congregants. For many African Caribbean Pentecostals the degree of spiritual insight is not simply measured by biblical hermeneutics but as indicated by the presentation of those ideas. Speaking of African American preaching, which in this sense can be equally applicable to the British Caribbean context, LaRue (2011, p. 418) says although it has its imperfections it continues to be regarded in many circles 'as the most vibrant, imaginative and communicatively effective preaching on the scene today', but there are plenty of 'questionable antics' and even 'heresy'. The latter point is significant, especially as the laity tend to regard clergy as authoritative interpreters of Scripture.

Pentecostal preaching in general can be charged with being a site for undiscriminating hermeneutics. Asamoah-Gyadu (2004) identifies 'proof-texting' as an approach to preaching whereby biblical texts are often taken out of context, which may produce erroneous views on theological matters. Consequently, Pentecostal hermeneutics has been disparaged and writers such as Fee (2006) claim that Pentecostals are known for their weak hermeneutics. Pentecostal ministers globally sometimes misinterpret the meaning of certain biblical texts due to a lack of proper grammatico–historical exegesis, which takes into account the common rules of grammar, syntax and the historical context.

Nonetheless, many Pentecostals including African Caribbean clergy will not want merely to accept reductionist hermeneutics focusing on grammatico–historical exegesis to the exclusion of a pneuma–centric one. Any robust application of hermeneutics will not obliterate the major tenets of Pentecostalism. As Adedibu (2012, p. 139) states: 'In recent years there has been much exegesis from the pens of black majority churches in Britain, but this is a reflection of a global renaissance amongst Pentecostal scholars.'

However, the accusation levelled at Pentecostals of having an uncritical theology is not without merit, and reticence about certain types of theological education is undoubtedly a factor (although in America this is not necessarily the case, evidenced by the plethora of seminaries and institutions such as Oral Roberts University). As previously mentioned, some Pentecostal ministers in Britain are untrained theologically, but increasingly many are gaining relevant qualifications. For African Caribbean Pentecostal clergy, the lack of theological education impacting on their hermeneutics must be seen in light of the wider debate surrounding the academic performance of black Caribbean students, particularly males. Many of the first generation were, by and large, uneducated and many of the second fared little better in compulsory education (see the Rampton Report 1981). Fortunately, some acquired academic qualifications as young or mature adults (Rhamie 2007). Given that many of the first-generation preachers, overwhelmingly male, did not possess formal theological literacy skills, this led to a dependence on oratorical ability rather than systematic theological knowledge. It can be argued that despite increased theological educational provision for the second generation, they are very often not in a position to sustain courses of study, due to financial constraints. Furthermore, African Caribbean people as a group tend to be at the lower end of the social strata economically irrespective of their academic credentials. Another important factor is that these ministers invariably lead churches in deprived urban areas, thus affecting their remuneration and thereby impeding higher education aspirations.

5 Plenary view of the Bible and interpreting biblical texts

Regardless of the extent of theological education, hermeneutically Pentecostals tend to have a plenary verbal inspiration view of the Bible, a belief that every word is inspired by the Holy Spirit of God. Even though Pentecostals believe that the Scripture is divinely inspired, it can be argued that human beings do not always interpret it accurately, irrespective of their theological persuasion. African Caribbean Pentecostals have an extremely high view of the Bible and Sturge (2005) points to the pre-eminence of Scripture for black Pentecostals who see the written word as having similar characteristics to the incarnate Word, Jesus Christ (John 1). Sturge highlights the supremacy of Scripture for this group, substantiated by a key verse in 2 Timothy 3.16 (KJV/NJKV) which states, 'All Scripture is given by inspiration of God.' The view of the Bible as infallible or inerrant does not imply that various versions of Scripture are error free. It is precisely this reason why many Pentecostals globally place the Authorised Version of the Bible, popularly referred to as the King James, as the foremost text, viewed by some as the version that is least contaminated. Also, this was the version that was first introduced historically around the globe. Some contemporary African Caribbean ministers, including myself, often encourage congregants to read other versions, but in most churches preachers during sermons tend to quote from the King James. The communicative patterns of African Caribbean interlocutors utilizing metaphoric and symbolic language make certain texts from the King James which sound poetic in nature easier to retain and recite, corresponding to the lyrical quality of their speech.

LaRue (2011) confirms that black preachers view the Scriptures, although composed of different materials, as the revelation of the narrative of the history of salvation. God is believed to be the author of the Bible, and the Scriptures, though written by several authors, speak in some direct way on God's behalf. Thus, by extension, God may be seen as the real author. The idea that certain texts can be relegated is abhorrent to the majority of African Caribbean Pentecostal preachers. LaRue rightly asserts that black preachers believe that the attentive interpreter can hear God speaking directly through the text and there is very often convergence between the preacher and the events of the text. He goes on to state:

> Blacks are often not given credit for the nuancing they do in this paradigm. To say that one expects to be addressed by God through Scripture is not to suggest that Scripture must be taken literally in all its parts. Instead, the search that drives the desire to understand and interpret the Scriptures grows out of the belief that somehow, in some manner, God is speaking through a particular text. The finds of historical–

> critical research are of immense benefit to blacks in their quest to hear the voice of God. Blacks simply refuse to relegate that voice strictly to the historical past. (p. 1137)

Sturge (2005, p. 133) argues convincingly that an all-powerful God has the divine ability to communicate his thoughts and wishes to his children. Although this view should not be incredulous, it can, as he points out, create a 'self-generating hermeneutic' according every verse the same worth. Unfortunately, the fundamentalist position adopted by Pentecostals has too often been synonymous with indoctrination and lack of criticality, and confused with non-negotiable essential Christian beliefs that as Sturge rightly states should be the basis for those professing the Christian faith. The Pentecostal tendency to imbibe a literalist approach in their hermeneutics can lead to selectivity of certain biblical texts without sufficient consideration for the context of the passage, but African Caribbean Pentecostals, as Sturge (2005, p. 133) articulates, are not literalist, theologically speaking. As he states:

> The nature of their culture has created a heightened sense of symbolism and metaphor. There is no doubt when Scripture speaks about 'break[ing] up your fallow ground' (Jeremiah 4:3) this is understood to mean 'preparing our hearts for a renewed fruitful and living encounter and relationship with God' ... some preachers rely heavily on allegory.

It must be emphasized that exegesis of the biblical text is not culturally neutral or objective and within African Caribbean Pentecostalism it can be identified by culturally embedded practices that inform hermeneutical frames. In that sense, employing contextual theology could enhance our understanding of the homiletic practices of African Caribbean Pentecostal clergy.

It is helpful to invoke Ukpong's (2001) inculturation hermeneutics postulating the role of the Bible reader's context in the hermeneutical approaches to the African Caribbean social cultural context. Writing about African biblical scholarship,

Ukpong advocates that epistemological privilege should be given to the ordinary reader (and ordinary Pentecostal clergy). Hence, 'the primacy of the reading activity is located not among theologians working in isolation but among theologians working among communities of ordinary people – it is the ordinary people that are accorded the epistemological privilege' (p. 20). It could be argued that a hermeneutics grounded in theology drawing on other relevant disciplines such as history and sociology, coupled with robustly documenting the voices of African Caribbean Christians and their interpretation of the sacred text might be beneficial for both ministers and biblical scholars.

To that end, writers such as Beckford advocate that theologians must consider black experiences to engage with theology. Adedibu (2012) explains that black Pentecostals approach Scripture with various pre-understandings and suppositions that are inextricably linked with prior experience, which might implicate the interpretation of the text. Personal experience qualitatively impacts on how we all interpret the Bible. Mullings (2009, 2010) presents an innovative framework and argues that given the primacy of the Bible for African Caribbean Christians in Britain, it is important that a critical reading of biblical texts should be undertaken through the lens of their experiences. She introduces black biblical hermeneutics by invoking the work of African American Hebrew scholar Randall Bailey, who outlines the ways in which the Bible has been interpreted from a colonial and dominant perspective. She utilizes and makes a plea for the Jamaican vernacular and vernacular hermeneutics for critical engagement of the Scriptures, 'through an assessment of the Bible Society of the West Indies' work, "A Who Run Tings?" – translated passages of the Gospels into Jamaican (otherwise known as patois)' (Mullings 2010, p.2). The relevance of the Jamaican language has already been discussed in Chapter 3 relating to preaching. The Jamaican voice and how it represents biblical themes are critical in understanding the hermeneutics found in black Caribbean Pentecostal churches.

6 Preaching in context

Preaching in context refers to the circumstances out of which preaching emerges. Preaching does not operate in a social, cultural or theological vacuum but is appropriated in particular contexts, and African Caribbean Pentecostal preaching has to be seen within the broader spectrum of Pentecostalism historically. Scholars such as Robert Mapes Anderson view early Pentecostalism as arising from the extreme social tensions among the poor and dispossessed caused by the shift from an agrarian to an industrial society. He argues that their belief in the imminent, apocalyptic return of Jesus Christ brought order to chaotic lives and alleviated social pressures. Similarly, the first generation of Caribbean Pentecostals who inherited a heaven-bound theology experienced arduous circumstances resulting from the post-slavery and post-colonial societies from which they came. This theology is also reflected in many of the Jamaican 'old-time' choruses demonstrated in the examples below – apart from the fourth one, which can also be found in the African American context:

Chorus 1

My home is in heaven just waiting for me
And when I reach there how happy I'll be
My home is in heaven, no rent to pay
My Jesus paid it, paid it all for me.

Chorus 2

I know where I am going, I know
I know where I am going, I know
Joy bells are ringing, happy children are singing
I know where I am going, I know.

Chorus 3

I'm on my way to heaven's land and I know I never will
turn back
By the grace of God, march until I win I know I never will
turn back ...
And when I reach that home above, what a happy time that
will be
Angel gonna bow their wing and saints are gonna sing
around the throne of God
I'm on way to heaven's land ...

Chorus 4

We'll soon be done with troubles and trials
In that home on the other side
I'm gonna shake my hands with elder
I'm tell God's people good morning
I'm gonna sit down beside my Jesus
I'm gonna sit down and rest a little while.

The second-generation preachers are attempting to reconcile the heaven-bound thinking of their forebears with living in the here and now of contemporary society. For example, the Black Theology forums organized by The Queen's Foundation, Birmingham explore a range of topics evidenced in a recent paper: 'Preparing the Black Church for the 21st Century' presented by Revd Dr Paul C. Stewart, a pastor from the Church of God of Prophecy.

7 Preaching Against Worldliness

In preparation for the return of Christ, early Pentecostal preachers expressed disapproval of activities considered to be worldly and thereby sinful, such as consuming alcohol or smoking tobacco and attending bars. Instead they encouraged the pursuit of sanctification, holiness and uncompromised devotion to God. African Caribbean Pentecostal clergy remain committed to these ideals and members are advised to refrain from 'worldly' or social entertainment such as 'clubbing'.

A popular 'old-time' chorus that is sung in contemporary African Caribbean Pentecostal churches illustrates this view.

Good bye world. I'll stay no longer with you
Good bye pleasures of sin. I'll stay no longer with you
I've made up my mind to go God's way for the rest of my life
I've made up my mind to go God's way for the rest of my life.

Increasingly among the younger generation, there is a certain amount of liberality pertaining to participating in certain social activities. It is not unusual for African Caribbean Pentecostals to attend the cinema, which was viewed with disdain some 30 years ago. However, the holiness roots of Pentecostalism with its emphasis on being 'separated from the world' has been maintained, reflected in the often quoted biblical verse by preachers to '... come out from among them, and be ye separate' (2 Corinthians 6.17 KJV).

8 Attire as signifiers

Moreover, the first Pentecostals at Azusa Street and the successive generations also believed that sanctification was not only displayed inwardly by the Spirit but also outwardly by the clothing worn, especially by women. Restrictions relating to dress have their antecedents in the Holiness dress codes of the nineteenth century. In several white Pentecostal/Charismatic churches in Britain there no longer appears to be an emphasis on female attire but this is not the case for African Caribbean Pentecostals, evidenced by the numerous discussions and references in preaching on the topic. According to Beckford (2013, p. 122) attire is another way that black Pentecostals inscribe sanctification on church culture and both formal and casual wear is a 'visual sign' of the sanctified life.

It was only some 20 years ago that female members during

main worship services in churches such as New Testament Church of God had to cover their hair, by wearing a scarf or hat. Hat-wearing remains a requirement in churches such as Bethel Apostolic First United church, based on the Pauline injunction of 1 Corinthians 11.3–16 concerning head covering for women in public worship; it can be argued that this is a misreading and misapplication of the cultural context of the Scripture. In some churches, the clergy and church 'mothers' (a term used to describe elderly women) still discourage women from wearing certain clothes such as trousers, cosmetics and jewellery, so that they can be distinguished from their non-Christian counterparts. Much of this has changed in many African Caribbean contemporary churches and the dress code is a lot more relaxed; however, there remains an unwritten code that one should not wear provocative or revealing clothes if one professes to be a committed Christian, and it is not unusual for both male and female preachers to remind women of how they should be dressed based on 1 Timothy 2:9, which states that women should dress modestly. The popular African American female preacher, Prophetess Dr Junita Bynum, in a recent Facebook post, expressed forcefully her distaste for some Christian women who wear 'tight clothes' in sacred spaces. Several black Pentecostals globally applauded her comments, yet as Aldred (2005) points out these Pentecostal churches are sites for 'ostentatious' dressing.

Reference to attire in preaching is codified for the 'sanctified woman', reflecting the commonly held view that a Christian woman should be distinguished from an 'unsaved' woman by their dress. Butler's (2007) brilliant historical study of African American women in the Church of God in Christ (GOCIC) in North America highlights that dress reveals theological inclination, particularly towards sanctification. Sanctified dressing is perceived as discouraging unwanted male attention, and symbolizes sexual purity and consecration. Clothing represents two functions: the first being a disjuncture from the world and the second embodies the idealized 'holy' woman. The discourses on women's clothes can be interpreted as sites for oppressive patriarchal practice that is plausible, but authors such as Toulis

(1997) draw attention to the complex gendered relationships in the African Caribbean community where women wield some influence. Furthermore, the ascribed low status of black women in mainstream society on both sides of the Atlantic, relatively speaking, possibly heightens for some the modelling of holiness through dress and deportment (Butler 2007). Perhaps the discussion could also be viewed from another angle, in that some women's fashion in modern societies is often represented in ways that objectify women, fuelling a hyper-sexualized consciousness, and in this sense reference to women's clothing in preaching can also be interpreted as a counterculture to this pervasive normative phenomenon.

9 Life situation and serial preaching

From the latter years of the twentieth century to the present, the focus in Pentecostal preaching has shifted away from an overemphasis on end-time messages and worldliness to some extent. This is possibly to deflect from the charge that Pentecostals were 'so heavenly minded they were of little earthly use'. Within the African Caribbean context, there have been vociferous calls for African Caribbean preachers to respond to contemporary social, economic and political challenges facing their community. Though the otherworldly messages encoded in Pentecostalism still inform preaching, it is remodelled in life situation and serial preaching. Life situation preaching is associated with the work of Revd Harry Emerson Fosdick, who regarded preaching and personal counselling as a means to address issues that are 'disrupting lives, troubling minds and burdening consciences' (Newton 2016, p. iv). While attempting to address personal issues, it runs the risk of not preaching the Bible as a whole. Serial preaching, on the other hand, is based on a series of themes or topics such as the kingdom and is expedient as congregants are informed of the subject in advance. Homilies in several African Caribbean churches inculcate both life situation and serial preaching and a vast array of topics are presented, ranging from money to the family and relationships, pertinent to living in the here and now. However, there appears to be a lack of lucid expository preaching on issues impacting on the African Caribbean community, such as the high rates of teenage pregnancy, the increase in gang culture and the preponderance of single women, especially in the church. Though areas of concern to ministers there is a need for a lucid biblical theology to address some of these matters.

10 Influences of prosperity theology

Significantly, some of the second and third generation preachers are influenced by the North American prosperity theology or gospel (see Bowler, 2013). The prosperity gospel, whose origins are in the Word of Faith movement, has had a profound impact on the global Pentecostal/Charismatic tradition including African Caribbean Pentecostalism. Critics often portray the prosperity message as preying on marginalized groups with the purpose of financially benefiting its advocates. The 'name it and claim it' identification of prosperity theology reveals the disdain given to this position. Sturge (2005) makes a valid point by explaining that this message should not be totally disregarded, despite some of its unsavoury aspects such as the excessively opulent lifestyle of some of its promoters. It does respond to a fundamental human question – what does God who is all-powerful have to say to the poor and socially marginalized? In that sense, according to Sturge, prosperity is similar to liberation theology in its intent but where the two differ is in their responses to social, economic and political structures. Whereas followers of prosperity theology lean towards the view that capitalist systems can be utilized for individual transformation, liberationists tend to identify with the poor and attack the system which breeds oppression.

The preaching discourse found in some independent African Caribbean churches attempts to replicate the prosperity theology of African American and Euro-American Pentecostal-type mega-churches established by charismatic preachers such as Creflo Dollar and Rod Parsley. These churches provide a fertile ground for the germination of the American 'seed sowing', harvesting 'abundant blessings' of prosperity in health and wealth, and more so, as many well-known tele-evangelists are often invited to Britain as guest speakers. It could be postulated that the future generation of African Caribbean Pentecostal clergy may become immersed in the 'prosperity gospel', and only time will tell. Based on my observations, it is unlikely to be the case as prosperity theology appears to be rooted in the 'American dream'. In Britain, there is no direct equivalent. In addition, social mobility in the United States resulting in a sizeable and distinct African American middle-class population is in contrast to reports of British Caribbean professionals, who express 'reluctance' and 'ambivalence' about occupying a dual position of being both black and middle class despite their emergence (Rollock et al. 2015). Similarly, the limited career opportunities afforded to working-class African Caribbean people (Clark and Drinkwater 2007) may well stem the full tide of the prosperity gospel within the British context, in spite of the prosperity themes within preaching.

Summary

The origin of Pentecostal preaching is located in the African America context emerging from the African oral tradition. I identified ten major areas in the homiletics of African Caribbean preaching, including the expressive and performative nature of preaching; deductive versus inductive sermons; approaches to sermonic preparation and delivery; Pentecostal hermeneutics and theological education; plenary view of the Bible and interpreting biblical texts; preaching in context; preaching against worldliness; attire as signifiers; life situation and serial preaching, and influence of prosperity theology.

Preachers communicate theological themes through a range of expressive behaviours that are culturally familiar to congregants. Sermonic preparation, combining a linear and episodic method, provides opportunities for flexible engagement with the Scriptures and interaction with the Holy Spirit. The hermeneutical approach of Pentecostalism in general can sometimes result in biblical texts being taken out of context. The preference for the Authorised Version of the Bible by these clergy ties to the metaphoric language of African Caribbean interlocutors. In this Pentecostal sphere, preaching in context historically centres on the challenges experienced by the Windrush generation who came from post-slavery and post-colonial societies with its attendant challenges. This has led to an eschatological or other-worldly view reflecting the theology of the founding fathers of Pentecostalism. Preaching on worldliness, and clothes as signifiers of sanctification are inherent, but there has been a shift contemporarily to life situation and serial preaching. The prosperity message has infiltrated the theology of African Caribbean Pentecostalism but whether or not it will be fully realized in Britain is yet to be seen.

Reflection and activities

- What are the challenges to the episodic approach to preaching proposed by David Buttrick?
- How might clergy who utilize the lectionary benefit from the approach to preaching adopted by second-generation African Caribbean Pentecostal clergy?
- In what ways might Pentecostal/Charismatic clergy benefit from lectionary preaching?
- Interpreting the Bible is challenging for both clergy and laypersons. What have you found to be the most appropriate approach to reading the Bible?
- Consider the differences between life situation and serial preaching. Examine the advantages and disadvantages of each type of preaching.
- What do you think might be the challenges for presenting the Christian faith to congregants in contemporary churches through life and serial preaching?

PART TWO

Tools

5

Artistic Oratory in African Caribbean Pentecostal Preaching

Part 1 of this book centred on the historical background of African Caribbean Pentecostalism and included the structural features of their language and the hermeneutics of their homiletics. The focus for Part 2 will be on the stylistic components of speech employed in African Caribbean Pentecostal preaching. This will examine the ways in which different elements of the linguistics, that is lexis, syntax, etc., combine to create a variety of effects; and also review Hymes' (1972) advice that the communicative habits of the entire community have to be considered in analysing the operations of language within any given social group. In this chapter preaching as an artistic form will be examined as a part of the African communication system (ACS) utilized by black people in various geographical locations. It will discuss the range of stylistic devices of preaching including improvisation, creative use of language, proverbial expression, oral narrative and dramatic presentation of self. The term black preaching as a point of reference will follow its usage in the literature reflecting some of its shared stylistic features found in varied Christian denominations especially in the diaspora. Despite these parallels, the discussion and sermonic exemplars for this chapter will largely be confined to the African Caribbean Pentecostal tradition in Britain.

Black preaching?

It is relevant at this point to clarify the term black preaching. This type of preaching is not merely a description of ethnicity.

Though often culturally identifiable with black preachers in the Pentecostal/Charismatic tradition, and in America the Baptists, it is illustrated in the preaching of Euro-American Pentecostals/Charismatics such as Cheryl Brady, Paula White and Rod Parsley. Hispanic ministers such as Samuel Rodriguez also utilize a black style of preaching. Moreover, there are individual diasporans on both sides of the Atlantic that do not wish to label their preaching as 'black' and as Thomas (2016, p. 34) suggests: 'there is no litmus test of orthodoxy for theoreticians and practitioners of black preaching to label or define themselves as "black preachers". Black preaching is a field and there are many valid points and perspectives, and no one size or shoe of orthodoxy fits all.'

Oratory in Africa and the Diaspora

As previously indicated it would appear that several African societies place a high value on the spoken word, reflecting a similar attitude among black people in the Americas, the Caribbean and Britain. Support for this idea comes from an understanding of the pre-slavery background entailing the concept of Nommo, the mystical power of the spoken word. Nommo is an integral aspect of the African worldview, necessary to bring life into being and to give individuals control over their daily circumstances. Oratory as a literary art form is embedded in many West African countries, the ancestry of many slaves. One commentator, R. A. Freeman, on his visit to Ashanti, stated in 1888 that: 'The art of oratory is in West Africa carried to a remarkable pitch of perfection ... These oratorical displays appear to afford great enjoyment to the audience, for every African native is a born orator and a connoisseur of oratory' (cited in Wolfson 1958, p. 193). Consequently, the tapestry of language remains interwoven into the fabric of many African societies and is both energetic and aesthetically pleasing. African diasporans have retained this vibrant oration and despite the prominence of the European model language, the ACS persists.

The African-derived oral tradition has also been reported in academic research on Caribbean literary writers such as Edward

Kamau Braithwaite who sequence elements of Africanisms in their writings (Cudjoe 2001; Sindoni 2009). The emphasis on orality, the potency of the word and the communication strategies have produced a unique style of speaking which is also manifested in preaching. Smitherman (1977, p. 90) describes the sacred style of black churches as: 'That in which the content and religious substance has been borrowed from West Judaeo–Christian tradition but the communication of that content – the process – has remained essentially African.'

Oratory in preaching

The communication style and skills of black preachers have been well documented. For instance, they are discussed in Africa by Nhiwatiwa (2012), in the Caribbean by Kuck (2007), in America by Mitchell (1970, 1990), Kenyatta (2011), LaRue (2011, 2016) and Thomas (2016). In Britain the oratorical flair of African Caribbean preachers are featured in the writings of Sutcliffe and Tomlin (1986), Tomlin (1988, 1999, 2014), and Thomas (2014). The black church as the most powerful institution offers an important platform for the development and display of oration.

With reference to African American preaching, transposed to the African Caribbean context, LaRue (2011, p. 1425) says that oral language is an extremely valued communicative tool and a 'highly sought-after art among young and old black preachers alike'. This 'love of language' can be found in a cross-section of black preaching styles and observed in various Christian denominations. For instance, Wilkinson (1993) reports that some Anglican parishioners in the city of Birmingham believe that black Anglican preachers have a more powerful delivery than their white counterparts. The brilliance of Revd Dr Martin Luther King's 'I Have a Dream' speech marks it as a prime example of an African–American sermonic text within the Baptist tradition. The virtuosity of black preaching was attested by the 'Power of Love' sermon by Bishop Michael Curry, who 'stole the show' at the wedding of Prince Harry and Meghan Markle in May 2018.

'Folk sermons' and Pentecostal preaching

It is important to shed light on the source of oratory of Pentecostal preaching, apart from the African linguistic retentions, by focusing on the style of 'folk sermons' shared by black and white evangelicals alike during the Great Awakening. These sermons were built on formulaic structure based on stock phrases, verses and passages that preachers committed to memory; their features were:

> characterised by repetition, imagery, dramatic use of voice and gesture and a range of oratorical devices. The sermon began with normal conversational prose, then built to a rhythmic cadence, regularly marked by the exclamations of the congregation, and climaxed in a tonal change accompanied by shouting, singing, and ecstatic behaviour. The preacher, who needs considerable skill to master this art, acknowledged not his own craft but rather the power of the Spirit, which struck him and set him on fire. (LaRue 2011, p. 1491)

It is fascinating that these aspects of preaching by both black and white evangelicals of yesteryear have been preserved among second- and third-generation African Caribbean Pentecostals in modern British society.

It is apparent that Pentecostalism as a global phenomenon has meant, as Kay (2015) observes, international migration or travel, which has enhanced the synthesis of cultural styles. African preachers throughout Europe preach in various parts of Asia, Australian preachers in, say, Hong Kong and British ones, both black and white, in North America. The media including social media routinely stream live preaching that can also be watched on YouTube. Despite the impact of global networks on the style of Pentecostal preaching, African Caribbean preaching, as we will further demonstrate, is distinct.

The artistic oratory of black preaching in general has been widely acclaimed, and many ministers within the Pentecostal tradition in particular are held in high esteem partly because of their verbal dexterity. Based on my observations a fair number use language in ways that can hold an audience for up to one hour and sometimes beyond, an hour being the average timeframe for sermons in most black Pentecostal churches. Sermons tend to be dynamic in delivery and preachers deemed as excellent such as Bishop John Francis and his wife, co-pastor Penny Francis, are able to captivate their audience with their rhetorical flair and in-depth biblical study.

Nhiwatiwa (2012) reminds us that the language of the clergy should be informed by the culture and experiences of the people. Preachers often inculcate the speech patterns of their peers and in this sense African Caribbean preaching can be described as contextual for it utilizes the language of the group. Let us now turn to the linguistic strategies of preachers that depend on the communicative style of the ACS.

Improvisation

Okpewho (1992, p. 96) observes improvisation in several African societies, calling this device digression, whereby the oral performer departs temporarily from the main theme of the subject of a story to address something else or to comment on an issue which may be closely or remotely connected to the main subject. Improvisation is apparent in the way that preachers are able to highlight the main points of their sermons by means of deviation.

In my (1988) early research on black preaching, I observed improvisation in the discourse of both white British and black Caribbean Pentecostal ministers under study, but noted the cultural differences in the responses of congregants with the former being much more muted. In the African Caribbean churches, the ecstatic spiritual reactions to the Holy Spirit recall the impulses from Africa, critical to the development of improvisation. The first generation of Caribbean preachers, for example Pastor Peterking from the Bethel Apostolic First United Church in Dudley, West Midlands, heavily relied on improvisation. Given their lack of training in homiletics and hermeneutics, it could be readily employed as a linguistic tool.

Attention was drawn in Chapter 4 to sermon preparation and presentation. Preachers from the Windrush generation were primarily oral, relying on memory. Second- and third-generation clergy tend to prepare their sermons by writing notes aided by a range of biblical commentaries and extra-biblical sources, etc. More academically inclined ministers in their sermon presentations invariably refer explicitly to a range of theological ideas they have researched. A common practice for some clergy belonging to other Christian traditions is to present the homily by actually reading from carefully prepared sermon notes. In contrast, whatever the preparation format, these Pentecostal preachers tend not to read the whole of their sermon script. Even the most well-prepared sermons contain a great deal of improvisation or spontaneity, which is an integral feature of the ACS and suggestive of an oral–written tradition. Of the preachers studied by Mitchell (1990, p. 126), practically all used their manuscripts extremely well but 'engaged in interludes of completely spontaneous elaborations or illustrations. On the whole these were very plainly more effective than the passages that were read.' Incidentally, Bishop Michael Curry said in an interview with Piers Morgan, on the television programme *Good Morning Britain*, that there were a few 'ad libs' in his sermon at the wedding of Prince Harry and Meghan Markle.

The use of improvisation in black preaching, despite theological education, underscores the significance of this device. It is the unwavering belief that the Holy Spirit is central to the sermon leading up to the preaching act itself that elicits improvisation. The preparation and delivery of the famous 'I Have a Dream' speech by Revd Dr Martin Luther King vividly illustrates the belief in the guidance of the 'Spirit', and the implementation of improvisation as an oration strategy among black preachers. Apparently, King typically prepared his sermons and political speeches by jotting down a few notes on the back of a church bulletin before speaking, relying on improvisation according to the leading of the Holy Spirit. In his speech, King also improvised the concluding remarks, after being spurred on by the gospel singer Mahalia Jackson, who shouted 'Tell them about the dream, Martin!' King looked out over the crowd and as he explained later in an interview 'all of a sudden this thing came to me that I have used – I'd used many times before, that thing about "I have a dream" – and I just felt that I wanted to use it here.'

Similarly, in relation to improvised text in sermons, African Caribbean Pentecostal preachers also say that 'something just came to me'. Revd Jackie Reid makes use of improvisation in the sermon entitled: 'How'. In the first part of the following excerpt she presents from the written script, to a great extent, but in the second part improvisation is apparent:

> Many years ago I used to watch the TV programme for kids called HOW. In the programme it showed you how many things came into existence. Do you know that God has given man the supernatural ability whether or not they are born again to do many things; think about it. Think about all the inventions. Think about the TV; how do we get the signal and hear someone speak? How do we see people on the TV and it looks as if they are with us. How do we talk to someone thousands of miles away on the telephone?
>
> How do we plug in the many devices we have and how does it work through the electricity? and some of us as my mum would say 'burn out the current'. How does the computer work? How do we send emails? How do we save documents? Yes I know there are many principles scientifically but who gave man the knowledge? How did it happen? We know God gave man the knowledge.
>
> Wait, wait, wait a minute. Oh Lord, the plane. For the plane to take off there is lift. I don't have a clue about lift. I am just getting a download that there is the law of lift. The plane has to lift.
>
> Have we got anyone in the congregation who has studied physics?
>
> [Someone raises their hand to affirm and explain the law]
>
> *Woww* ... [paralinguistic feature].

Apparently, Revd Jackie was not conversant with the law of lift as an aerodynamic force and the concept 'came to her' while she was preaching, hence the remark 'I am just getting a download'.

The popular second-generation itinerant preacher, Pastor Mark Liburd, describes a sermonic encounter where he 'felt led' to change his entire 'message'.

> I am learning how to feel comfortable in what you already know ... Having the faith and confidence to utilize the gift God has given you. God may require you to change the direction of your sermon. One time, I was going to preach on worship. I had an internal dialogue with the Holy Spirit and felt I had to change the direction of the message ... I had to go out (of the main service) find the text and quickly read it. I knew the story but had to regain the story in my mind. I preached on the field of blood. How Judas' greed fuelled his action to buy 'the field of blood' resulting in dire consequences. Change means trusting God to change the sermon if necessary. (Personal communication)

As previously mentioned African Caribbean Pentecostal clergy believe that the homily including topic, theme, content, etc., can be revised by the leading of the Holy Spirit.

Sometimes preachers improvise by inviting individual congregants to role-play as a means of further clarifying an idea. It is typically unrehearsed and congregants often have no foreknowledge of the theme or idea to be role-played as it is a spontaneous request. Take the sermon on 'Grace' by Pastor Esther, where she illustrated the differences between law and grace. She used three people referred to here as A, B and C, to explain that the Mosaic Law entails intensive labour to gain righteousness. Person A had to work hard by tilling the ground with imaginary implements, person B was required to relax in their chair by leaning on person C who represented grace conferred to an individual by the Lord Jesus Christ. Throughout the demonstration, Pastor Esther provided a running commentary of each person's enactment without the use of notes and emphasized the key point that person B was able to produce a fruitful Christian life through depending on the Lord, person C. Improvisation through role-play is often used as an exegetical approach to aid understanding of a theological point.

Not only is improvisation evident in spoken texts but it is also entrenched in black musical and singing genres such as Soca, Reggae, Afrobeat, Jazz, Rap, etc. Speaking of African preachers, Nhiwatiwa (2012, p. 70) explains that they are expected to 'embellish the sermon with songs'. In fact, it is fairly common for preachers to improvise at the beginning, middle or end of sermons by singing or saying a verse of a gospel chorus, song or hymn. For example, the Jamaican bishop, Jackie McCullough at the Pentecostal Faith Holy Convocation, 2018 in Detroit, began her sermon with:

> I am Thine, O Lord, I have heard Thy voice,
> And it told Thy love to me;
> But I long to rise in the arms of faith
> And be closer drawn to Thee.
>
> Refrain
> Draw me nearer, draw me nearer blessèd Lord,
> To the cross where Thou hast died.
> Draw me nearer, nearer blessèd Lord,
> To Thy precious, bleeding side.

Bishop McCullough continued her introduction by stating: 'And here's my favourite verse':

> Consecrate me now to Thy service, Lord,
> By the power of grace divine;
> Let my soul look up with a steadfast hope,
> And my will be lost in Thine.

The bishop concluded the introduction to her homily by stating, 'If that's your desire give him a standing ovation tonight ...'

Improvisation reveals the artistic ingenuity of language use among black people across the sacred and secular domains.

Creative use of language

The creative use of language is one of the striking features of the ACS. Speakers in conversation will recreate words or phrases. The play on words or pun characterizes this stylistic device observed throughout Africa and diasporic communities and is prevalent in Pentecostal preaching as illustrated by the following two examples: 'God does not call the qualified; he qualifies the called.' This statement has circulated in several Pentecostal settings globally. 'Anything natural cannot take care of the supernatural' (Priscilla Shirer – Bible teacher, actress and author).

In the British context some of the words or phrases spoken by African Caribbean interlocutors derive from JC or the pronunciation is JC, and among the young, BBT. The examples below are casual conversations between myself and a couple of my friends, which demonstrate the creative use of language. The first sentence text is with Sharon and focuses on individuals not feeling as if they are succeeding in their Christian life. The background to the first dialogue is the biblical narrative recorded in 2 Samuel 9 of Mephibosheth, the late King Saul's grandson who was disabled and lived in a place called Lodebar. The successor king, David, informed Mephibosheth that he could obtain Saul's land as his inheritance and dine with him at his palace for the remainder of his life. In black preaching Lodebar is pronounced as 'Lowdabar'. In Pentecostal preaching generally, Lodebar symbolizes a Christian who is oblivious that they belong to the royal priesthood of King Jesus, as represented in the story of Mephibosheth. Sharon, therefore states:

> Lowdabar is like lower the bar but it is now time for Christians to raise the bar. We are tired of loooo de bar, lowering the bar. It is time for us to lift up the bar.

The second and third texts are with Pauline. The first describes her ability to be discreet:

> I do not tell the la, la, la, la, reh, reh, reh, and teh, teh, teh ... (JC)

The third centres on the need for individuals to experience transformation:

> I always say: 'you have to want to change to change' (BBT)

Preachers also draw on JC/BBT phrases at certain points in their sermons. Take the following sentence from a sermon on ministry by Pastor Mark Liburd:

> Our tings mash up and we crash.

Direct translation:

> Our tings (Our things)
> Mash up (have been destroyed)
> And we crash (cave in)

Thus rendering the above sentence to mean that we are sometimes unsuccessful in our endeavours and are left depleted and unable to continue.

The semantic meanings of words and phrases are altered and the re-created words do not form a part of the repertoire of the standard language. For instance, millennial preachers influenced by the African American urban Hip Hop culture (see Mocombe, Tomlin and Callender 2017) use certain phrases such as 'ride or die' meaning a person who remains loyal to their partner or friend at any cost, and 'popping' or 'slaying' to denote someone who is fashionable. Similarly, young black British people including preachers refer to the social media website Facebook as Facety Book. Facety is a JC term borrowed from the SE word feisty – a relatively small but lively and determined person or a sensitive and aggressive individual. Facety in JC has a negative connotation to mean someone who is impertinent. Facebook is sometimes used as a vehicle for offensive communication or in extreme cases for cyber bullying, hence the term facety book. The term FBI, which stands for Facebook Investigators, is also a popular phrase to describe inquisitive individuals who spend an inordinate amount of time on Facebook. Preachers also create words, which appear on social media. For example, Apostle Keenan Bridges in a recent Facebook live presentation (19 January 2018) used the term frien-emies, combining the words friend and enemies, to explain how individuals can have so-called friends who are actually akin to enemies.

On the media theme, the early Pentecostals' aversion to participating in worldly activities meant that subsequent generations did not watch television, which was perceived as promoting worldly values, and many Pentecostals remain reluctant to watch certain programmes, especially those with explicit sexual content. A fellow minister stated that his father, who himself was a pastor, prohibited the family from watching television and was possibly the reason for the phrases 'hell-ivision' and 'tell-lie-vision'. With the passage of time these phrases become obsolete, replaced by others.

Words are often recreated through changing the suffixes or word endings reflective of JC, so falsify is 'falseness', suffering, 'sufferation' and support referred to as backing, 'backative'. Words are also combined and are spoken in Pentecostal churches throughout Africa and its diaspora. Take the term 'fantabulous' from the combined words fantastic and fabulous. As a prelude to his sermon entitled: 'Elevated by the Power of God', Pastor Nathan Turner from the Rock New Testament Church of God in Birmingham, stated that the congregants looked 'fantabulous'.

Sermon titles also demonstrate the creative use of language, evidenced in the examples below:

What time is it? End time (Revd Grey)
Don't blame me blame yourself (Revd John Grey, son of the above)
Seeing Clearly (Pastor Peterking)
Stick to the Plan (Prophetess Tamika Pusey-Squire)
A Call to Remembrance (Bishop John Jackson)
Favour Ain't Fair (Bishop T. D. Jakes)
No more Sheets (Prophetess Junita Bynum)

The theme for a convention in Jamaica, 2017 was entitled: 'Bawl Out'. The word bawl is a JC wrod, derived from Old English, which has two meanings: firstly to cry loudly, and secondly to reprove in a loud voice or to rebuke sharply. The theme may be an exhortation for the Christian community to become more committed in practising their faith.

The use of similes and alliteration are important components of figurative language and it is common for preachers to employ these in their speech. Similes are used as in the following examples: 'Tight like glue and paper'; 'tight like drums skin'; 'tight like flint'; 'ugly like sin'. In Pentecostal preaching, alliteration is demonstrated in phrases such as 'Love the life you live and live the life you love', drawing on the reservoir of linguistic flow.

Tonal semantics and poetic rhetoric

The distinctive rhythmic nature and cadence of many interlocutors in the diaspora is a marker that appears to be an African import. Finnegan (2012, p. 6) notes the 'highly tonal nature of many African languages ... Tone is sometimes used as a structural element in literary expression and can be exploited by the oral artist in ways somewhat analogous to the use of rhyme or rhythm in written European poetry.' She observes that this stylistic aspect in African poetry, proverbs and 'drum' literature is often under-represented in written versions or studies of oral literature. Tone is clearly one that involves voice manipulation in subtle and effective ways in the process and presentation of delivery. Smitherman (1977, p. 134) calls this kind of verbal technique tonal semantics which:

> refers to the use of voice rhythm and vocal inflection to convey meaning in black communication. In using the semantics of tone, the voice is employed like a musical instrument with improvisations, riffs, and all kinds of playing between the notes. This rhythmic pattern becomes a kind of acoustical phonetic alphabet and gives black speech its songified or musical quality.

Tonal semantics in speech is hardly surprising as music forms an integral part of African and diasporic cultures and points to the rhythmic view of life, underpinning the African world view. Okpewho (1992, p. 90) explains that tonality is well represented in languages across Africa and is a notable feature of oral literature. Tonal semantics invariably utilizes repetition, which will be analysed in Chapter 7. Tonal semantics is not only confined to speech in the sacred domain. The oratory of Barack Obama is an obvious example of political discourse that has a distinctive prosody. In the sacred context, this device is often used to convey spiritual activities such as prayer. Take the extract of a sermon about prayer by Revd Chris Tunde Joda of Nigeria which demonstrates this device:

> God should be a God you can pray to and he can answer your prayer. He should be a God that you can talk to in the morning, talk to in the afternoon, talk to in the midnight hour and he can be as real to you as any other time.

Often exaggerated stress is placed either at regular intervals or on key words in a performance, in this case 'talk to'. Additionally, there is a play on certain words as can be seen in the following sentence from Pastor Creflo Dollar:

> Willpower without Jesus power will not be lasting power.

Here, through tonal semantics, Pastor Dollar explains that the power of Jesus supersedes human effort and ability and is an exhortation of the power of Jesus Christ over human tenacity. The manipulation of the voice range so that the speech has a rather rhythmic quality is also evident, for instance, in the preaching of the late Dr Benson Idahosa from Nigeria, Bishop T. D. Jakes from America, and Pastor Blair from Jamaica. In Britain tonal semantics can be seen, for example, in the sermons of Pastor Peterking, Bishop John Francis, Pastor Mark Liburd and Pastor Esther Bonsu.

Tonal semantics is closely related to poetic rhetoric and includes genres such as Hip Hop, Reggae and Freestyle poetry. Poetic rhetoric is demonstrated in phrases such as the following:

'Later will be greater' and 'Don't mess with the best until you can pass the test.'

Preachers often utilize poetic rhetoric in phrases which then become popularized as in the following examples below:

'The church is not a place of entertainment but amazement.'
'Man's extremities are God's opportunities.'
'The source of the force is the Holy Ghost.'
'Do not equate sin with the colour of my skin.'
'When God wills it, He builds it.'
'You're not going to die if you say Hi.'
'God does not call the qualified, he qualifies the called.'

Proverbs and imagery

Proverbs or proverbial expressions, also referred to as sayings, are an essential aspect of the ACS and are widely used in conversation. They have been discussed, for instance, in an African context by Finnegan (1970, 2012) and Okpewho (1992). In several West African societies, for instance, proverbs facilitate local and cultural knowledge. According to Nhiwatiwa (2012, p. 5), 'African authors have long acknowledged the role of proverbs in the African culture in general and in African preaching in particular.' In the diaspora they are a part of the inherited African linguistic culture and reflect English influences of the slavery era and are featured in the writings of Abrahams (1972), Watson (1991) and Jackson (1986, 2012). They can be demonstrated in the political arena, in conversations and of course in preaching.

The African Caribbean Member of Parliament, David Lammy, invoked a proverb in his impassioned speech to the House of Commons denouncing the former Home Secretary, Amber Rudd and Prime Minister Theresa May, for the deportation of some of the Windrush generation. Here is an extract from his speech:

> This is a day of national shame, and it has come about because of a hostile environment policy that was begun

under her Prime Minister. Let us call it like it is. If you lie down with dogs, you get fleas and that is what has happened with this far-right rhetoric in this country.

The proverb, 'If you lie down with dogs, you get fleas' means that if you associate with unpleasant individuals some of their misdemeanours will influence you to some degree. It would appear that a significant number of proverbs found in the Caribbean are centred on animals including the ones below:

What sweet nanny goat will run him belly.
(Even though the things nanny goat eats taste delicious, she may experience an upset stomach.) In other words many situations that at first seem attractive may have dire consequences.

Play with puppy, puppy lick you.
(It is advisable to have clear boundaries with children or they may behave inappropriately.)

Hog say to pig, pig what make yu mout so long,
pig sey hog you a grow you will fine out
(The baby pig said to its mother, 'Why is your mouth so long' [large], and the mother replied 'when you grow up you will find out'.)
Adults often say this proverb to young people, which means that experience and maturity teach about life's challenges.

Several members of the older Caribbean community in Britain are living storehouses of proverbs, utilizing them frequently in conversation, which ties in with the idea that age denotes wisdom.

Pentecostal preachers creatively weave proverbs or proverbial expressions into their sermons, and in the sacred realm the proverb about the pig can refer to the fact that spiritual insight or otherwise will become apparent when a young Christian matures in their faith. The first-generation preachers employed proverbs to enlighten, elaborate and to convey meaning dramatically and memorably. The following are three examples:

> If a thing is worth having, it is worth hearing (Pastor Peterking)
> Beauty is only skin deep (Pastor Peterking)
> See and blind, hear and deaf (Pastor Jackson)

Several younger ministers cite proverbs garnered from their elders. Pastor Isaiah-Raymond Dyer quotes a number of proverbs in a recent homily entitled: 'Anointed but in Animosity' (posted on Facebook on 9 February 2018). In Pentecostal circles the word 'anointed' can refer to individuals who are spiritual or who have a tremendous gift from God in, say, singing or preaching. The encompassing theme of his homily centres on the importance of highly gifted individuals developing Christ-like character or the fruit of the Spirit as expressed in Galatians 5.22, as opposed to exhibiting negative personality traits. He states that it is imperative for leaders to be aware of how they present themselves by inserting the proverb: 'The higher the monkey climb the more he is exposed'. (Other versions state: 'The higher the monkey climb the more you see his behind'.) In other words, success in relation to ministry can often lead to public scrutiny. He explains that conflicts are unavoidable and relays the popular Jamaican proverb, 'Tongue and Teet [teeth] must meet', which incidentally relies on tonal semantics. Pastor Isaiah-Raymond continues by stating 'there is a Jamaican saying, a no every pan wey a nak you fi jump to'. Note the basilect form of JC, that is, the grammatical components farthest removed from SE in the phrase 'a no every pan wey a nak' [not every pan that is knocking]. The proverb is loosely translated as: an individual should not 'jump' (dance) to every pan or musical implement. The term'jump' in this sense is the JC word for dance, rendering the sentence as: one should not dance to every type of music. Within the context of his homily, it could be interpreted as restraint in responding to conflict situations.

Nhiwatiwa (2012, p. 7) cautions that proverbs might change

with the passage of time and a preacher may use a proverb whose meaning does not have the same relevance for the hearer. Hudson (2018) outlines the significance of proverbs as a critical source of wisdom and a reservoir that Christian leaders can draw from, as they serve as a tool to enhance life skills. On the other hand, the ritualistic nature of proverbs can function as an affirmation of leadership roles and from a Foucauldian perspective they can be used as a vehicle to reinforce power.

Proverbs also rely on imagery. Take the popular phrase 'stop playing church', which admonishes individuals about the importance of pursuing a genuine Christian life. Pentecostals often use figurative language to present biblical texts, and as Brown Taylor (1993, p. 213) puts it: ' For preachers imagination is the ability to form images in the minds of their listeners that are not physically present to their senses, so that they find themselves in a wider world with new choice about who and how they will be.'

Such image-making is evocative, as can be seen in a quote of a sermon on God's benevolence by Pastor Peterking: 'You think is once or twice justice has knocked at my door but mercy answered'. Similarly, Pastor Mark in one of his sermons stated: 'we often want to put our mouth on the church', in other words to speak negatively about the church.

Take the following address delivered by Canon Joel Edwards at a marriage ceremony:

> God designed marriages. You know they say marriages are made in heaven. I'm not quite sure about that. Maybe, if they are, they're assembled on earth. After you leave the altar there is still a lot of work to be done ... they shouldn't be seen as Scandinavian pine furnishing, you know, which comes expensive and ready made, I think a feel of MFI stuff. Not because it's cheap but after you bought this stuff you have to go home and put it together. You have to go home and be ready to get down on your knees and look at the instructions together carefully and put it together.

He uses a typical Christian theme, the sacred nature of marriage, and examines its practical implications. He extends the popular adage that 'marriages are made in heaven but lived on earth' by drawing upon the analogy of self-assembled furniture. This kind of imagery, in which the ordinary things of life are spiritually elevated and removed, is typical of black Pentecostal delivery. He continues his address by highlighting the issue of mental strength of couples in marital relationships:

> I heard a quote from Mother Bell from COGIC [Church of God in Christ] at one time. I hope it was original because it was really good and she said, 'Now we really know who is stronger than whom don't we because when you look at it, man was made out of dust but woman was made out of bone. We often use bones to beat down dust [audience roars with laughter], but what God has given in our union is not a licence to do this but love.

Again, we see the powerful imagery of bones and dust to convey which gender really has the fortitude in the relationship. Reverend Edwards, like many preachers, uses imagery as a focal teaching point.

Oral narrative

Oral narrative, the art of storytelling, is another characteristic of diasporan culture and is a continuity of the African oral tradition. Tomlin (1999, p.116) states:

> In Africa and throughout the diaspora, storytelling is one of the entertainments provided for an evening of relaxation. Stories are often performed at social gatherings in both sacred and secular contexts. They are told on the street and in the home; adults in the community often gather the young ... indeed any social occasion could result in a story session.

Storytelling not only entertains but also teaches important lessons for life or aids in settling important matters of dispute.

It can also be used to transmit salient values and ideas such as 'it is ill-advised to oppress the weak'. It also functions to alleviate grief as in the stories often recounted during Nine Nights, social gatherings of bereaved family members and friends that often take place before the funeral of the deceased.

Oral narrative is also an integral element of black preaching style (Tomlin 1988). Stories are often biblical, sometimes imaginary and at other times based on true narratives of personal experiences; occasionally, they are stories which are well known. When Pentecostal clergy present homilies, their interaction with congregants is a communal event, reproducing traditional African religious practices where the story becomes the centre point and is interwoven in the lived experience of the congregants (Nhiwatiwa, 2012).

Voice, noise and dramatic presentation of self

The voice is one of the most powerful tools for preachers and how African Caribbean preachers use their voice is rather difficult to describe fully in writing. There is the nasal quality, the guttural effect, the sudden change of pitch, and the screeching sound. A widely held view of Pentecostals in general is that they preach in a rather loud voice although perceptions of volume and pitch in speech can be considered as a cultural construct. Some preachers do speak loudly, but it must be pointed out that black Pentecostals do not merely shout their way through sermons. There is a great deal of pitch control or voice variation, the nuances of which are captured by Raboteau (1995, pp. 143–4) who states:

> The preacher begins calmly, speaking in conversational, if oratorical and occasionally grandiloquent, prose; he then gradually begins to speak more rapidly, excitedly, and to chant his words and time to a regular beat; finally, he reaches an emotional peak in which the chanted speech becomes tonal and merges with the singing, clapping, and shouting of the congregation.

In the sermon 'Elevated by the Power of God' by Pastor Nathan Turner, for instance, his discourse was at first calm and measured but developed into a crescendo of noise utilizing more JC speech (see Appendix C).

In a study of interlocutors in Antigua, Reisman (1974) notes the use of creole as a departure from non-confrontation and decorum. He also believes it is related to the duality of cultural and linguistic ambiguity, that is, the function of creole and SE, with the former expressing African culture and the latter, English. This duality derives from the historical process of the Caribbean culture developed out of slavery and is remodelled. Therefore, two cultural strands are interwoven into a complex set of cultural and linguistic expression. According to Reisman a positive and negative aspect of low-status membership sometimes exists, marked by unruly, disorderly and non-English behaviour. Creole speech is associated with low status and remodelling in the linguistic sense increases the number of multi-meaning utterances characteristic of and identified by creole usage. An increase in creole or BBT for the second and third generations within the British context is manifested during moments of relaxation, expressiveness, involvement and unrestraint. Standard English on the other hand is perceived as maintaining standards of order, decorum and quietness and used in a non-confrontational manner. The Caribbean culture of which the church plays a pivotal role is often characterized by this underlying set of values (Tomlin, 1988). Often when preachers are making a strong point the volume of their voice increases and more creolized speech or BBT is likely to occur.

There is also an interrelationship between creole and making noise, which links to the sound and motion elements discussed in Chapter 2. Reisman goes on to explain that passionate discourses involving 'quarrelling' or argument breaks the norm of constraint and a connection is established between argument, creole and noise. Both creole and arguments are referred to as 'making noise'. He observes that Caribbean speakers seem to take great pleasure in making noise, but uses the word noise in the Elizabethan sense, to mean the noisy band of musicians or melodious sounds as opposed to the mere loud or disorderly component. He calls this contrapuntal in the sense that each voice has a tune that is maintained and that the voices often sing independently at the same time. As the Barbadian writer George Lamming so eloquently puts it: 'So I made a heaven of noise which is characteristic of my voice ... an ingredient of West Indian behaviours' (1960, p. 62). In African Caribbean Pentecostal preaching this contrapuntal dynamics of 'noise' is certainly evident.

Preachers also display presentation of self through a range of behaviours, which are culturally familiar to congregants. These responses comprise spasmodic movements, feet stomping, bouncing up and down, gesticulation of hands and hitting the pulpit. Preachers use varied facial expressions such as leaning the head to the side or protruding the lips. One common practice is stopping in the middle of a sentence for a few seconds when making an extremely important point, without completing the sentence, and the audience is expected to understand the meaning. Preachers sometimes vacate the lectern or podium by walking up and down the aisle while delivering their sermonic discourse. They will even place one hand on a congregant's shoulder or sometimes state the name of an individual congregant, which closes the psychological distance between themselves and the audience. Preachers convey their exposition in a number of stylized ways that are also dependent on their individual personalities.

The use of microphones, perspiring while preaching and performing a praise break are phenomena that contribute to the dramatic presentation of self and deserve some attention. Many preachers tend to hold the microphone up at around two inches away from their lips, which is customary for orators who speak to large crowds. During extremely intense preaching (usually marked by increased volume or loudness of speech), ministers tend to raise their arms and hold the microphone at a downward angle pointing it at the tip of their lips. This is especially the case among male preachers in North and Latin America and the African diaspora. Some African Caribbean and African American Pentecostals such as Bishop John Francis and Bishop T. D. Jakes perspire profusely, wiping the sweat sometimes streaming down their face with a flannel or large handkerchief. Sometimes, at such moments, they discard their jackets if they are formally attired. Female preachers such as Pastor Penny Francis and Bishop Jackie McCullough tend not to perspire to the same degree but also use a handkerchief, often lace. Ministers such as Bishop John Francis will sometimes perform a praise break while 'preaching up a storm'.

Summary

In general, diasporans have inherited the African oral tradition and of most concern in this chapter has been the preservation of those oral literacy practices by African Caribbean preachers in Britain. I have argued that the genesis of Caribbean Pentecostal homilies reflect some of the characteristics of 'folk sermons' produced by black and white preachers during the Great Awakening. There are shared features of preaching found among African heritage clergy across the Christian denominations due to the common language style. The stylistic features of the ACS evidenced in preaching include improvisation, creative use of language, tonal semantics or poetic rhetoric, proverbs, imagery, oral narrative, the use of voice, 'noise' and dramatic presentation of self. All these facets demonstrate the crafted art of preaching among African Caribbean Pentecostal clergy.

Reflection and activities

- Think of an orator that you most admire. What are some of the strategies that they implement to enliven their rhetoric presentation?
- Focus on a sermon that you are preparing. At what point could improvisation be utilized? You might want to practise this strategy in your sermon.
- Think of ways that you could include a song in your homily. You might want to choose one that is familiar to the congregants.

- The print media, for example newspapers, often have memorable or 'catchy' phrases to captivate their reading audience. List some memorable phrases you have heard in the past that could be included in a sermon you are preparing to present.

6

Intertwining the Preaching Act: Call and Response

This chapter will examine call and response, a fundamental feature of ACS, wherein an audience either echoes or adds to the utterance of a speaker or performer. There is evidence of highly stylized call–response behaviour in many black communities throughout the world including Britain. Not only are patterns of call–response observed in preaching but its manifestations are also evidenced in the liturgy.

A great deal of discussion centres on call–response in both sacred and secular contexts and much of the literature in this area derives from North America. Authors such as Smitherman (1977, 1996), Rosenberg (1988), Mitchell (1970, 1990), and Alim and Smitherman (2012) have written extensively on this particular stylistic feature. In Britain, there is emerging research on call–response behaviours in varied settings by scholars including Sutcliffe and Tomlin (1986), Callender (1997) and Tomlin (1988, 1999, 2014).

Call–response is one of the most important characteristics of the ACS. It is structurally stylized in sacred spaces although as Smitherman (1996) explains there is no rigid binary between the sacred and secular. The iconic 'I have a Dream' speech by Dr Martin Luther King gave the international audience a glimpse into call–response as a rhetorical device. It operates differently in speech because there are often a number of competing voices, unlike in preaching where the minister's voice predominates. Call–response is also ubiquitous in singing and music styles and central to the liturgy of Pentecostal churches, as discussed in Chapter 2.

Call–response is symptomatic of the highly interactive nature of the ACS. According to Smitherman (1977, pp. 104–8) the use of call–response reflects the traditional African worldview where the universe is rhythmic in nature and seen as composed of natural and supernatural forces which are both interactive and interdependent. As the basic organizing principle of speech, it enables African heritage people to achieve the unified state of harmony that is the basis of the traditional African worldview.

Mitchell (1970, p. 95) explains in his classic study on black preaching: 'The black style which includes the pattern of call and response, is very easily traceable to black African culture. Such response requires a participating audience.' In call–response, the audience or congregants respond to the preacher who, in turn, shapes his or her homily according to the audience's response. A favourable response will encourage the preacher to continue in the same or similar vein in their discourse; conversely, a muted response may suggest a change of course in the direction of the sermon or the implementation of new strategies to engage the audience. The interaction of the preacher and congregants is a highly sensitive one and indeed a symbiotic relationship. Such a symbiotic relationship depends to a large extent on shared experiences, core values and insights of biblical texts based on group solidarity. The purpose of this chapter is to explore the various forms and functions of call–responses primarily within sacred spaces.

Forms of call and response

Smitherman (1977, p. 107) provides one of the most descriptive and illuminating discussions on call–response. She identifies different kinds of responses: co-signing, on-T, encourager, repetition and completer-statements. Smitherman draws primarily on the African American context and I apply her analysis to a wider range of data. Smitherman's analysis is also extended to include the performer's cue (see Tomlin, 1999) and to a device called tracking. For the purposes at hand, the discussion will mainly be confined to the sacred context, highlighting specific examples principally from British data although examples from Africa, America and the Caribbean are also included, demonstrating the African substratum.

An analysis of the forms of call and response inculcates prosodic (stress and intonation patterns of an utterance), paralinguistic or aspects of speech not involving words, and non-verbal devices, which are used to cue audience participation. Moreover, the closely related strategy of overlapping often co-occurs with call–response behaviour and needs to be examined.

Co-signing

The most common type of response, co-signing, indicates agreement with the speaker's point. In the sacred setting there are comments such as 'Yes', 'Amen', 'Praise him', 'Praise the Lord', 'Tell it', 'Glory', 'Hallelujah', 'Hmhm'. Take the following example of co-signing from a first-generation minister, who is still preaching, Pastor Mavis Bailey from the International First Born Church of the Living God:

Pastor Mavis Bailey	When you experience the word became flesh ... and you see the manifestation of the word then nothing can stop you.
Congregational response	Amen, yes, hallelujah.
Pastor Mavis Bailey	No Amalekites, none of them will be able No Amorites, none of them will be able
Congregational response	Glory, amen, praise the Lord.
Pastor Mavis Bailey	None of the tites will be able ...

The responses from the congregation illustrate approval for the pastor and offer her feedback on her performance. Also, note creole influences in, 'when you experience the word became flesh' and the tonal semantics in the repetitious phrases 'No Amalekites, none of them will be able' and 'No Amorites, none of them will be able'. There is also word play on the suffix 'tites'.

On-T

Closely related to co-signing is what Smitherman (1977, p. 107) calls 'on-T'. This is an extremely powerful co-signing response acknowledging that something the speaker has said is 'dead on time' or accurate. Tomlin (1999) documents this more fully in other communities. In Sierra Leone and the Caribbean it is indicated by terms such as 'Woi' (fancy that), in America 'Who you telling?' (I have also heard this expression used by second-generation African Caribbean people), in Jamaica 'Ein ma/sa!' or 'behave/behave youself', and in Britain 'You know'. In the church context on-T can take the form of both verbal responses such as 'Yassuh!' and paralinguistic such as 'Mmmmm' and non-verbal responses including hand clapping, feet stomping, nodding the head vigorously and standing up or even jumping up to demonstrate agreement (Tomlin, 2014). If a preacher expresses views which speak directly to the experiences of the audience, a specific non-verbal cue is made in which the hand is raised to head level and then lowered in a singular or continuous pointing movement. This action signifies wholehearted approval for the preacher's points (Tomlin, 1999).

Encouraging

The third type of response identified by Smitherman is used to urge a speaker to continue in the same way in which they started. This device is used regularly in preaching to show that one is supporting the preacher. In West African Charismatic and Pentecostal churches, for example, the audience say 'Hallelujah' to encourage the preacher. In the African American Pentecostal and Baptist churches, members of the congregation who use encouraging interjections such as 'Glory to God', 'Take you time preacher' or 'Well', are referred to as being in the 'Amen Corner'. The term 'Well' is also used among the second and third generations in the British context. In both Jamaica and Britain 'Truly', 'Hmhm', 'Come on now preacher', 'Bless him Lord', 'Yea Lord', are some of the encouraging responses known as 'bearing up the preacher' (Tomlin, 1999, 2014). Interestingly, in Pentecostal churches in Africa and throughout the diaspora, the same encouraging strategies are used such as 'Preach', or 'Preach it', 'Yes Sir', or 'Yes', 'Come on now' and 'That's right/That's alright'.

Take the following example from Pastor Peterking, at the Bethel Apostolic First United church in Dudley, where he urges the congregation to involve God in future plans:

Pastor Peterking	Whenever we are planning make sure God is in it.
Congregational response	Yes sir, tell us.
Pastor Peterking	Don't try to jump in front of God …
Congregational response	No, no, bless him Lord.
Pastor Peterking	And don't follow too far behind.
Congregational response	Come on now preacher.

The preacher is spurred on in his delivery by the constant encouraging comments. The intensity of the audience response signals to the preacher that his points have been well received. As Rosenberg (1988, p. 65) points out, 'When an audience is responsive the preacher catches its enthusiasm.'

There are non-verbal cues, such as when both arms are outstretched, hands in motion beckoning the preacher. For example, in America, the phrase 'charging' is used, which I have also heard in Britain, when other spiritual leaders employ physical gestures to encourage a preacher in his/her delivery.

Repetition

A fourth type of response involves the repetition or partial repetition of the main speaker's call. Take the following appeal from Pastor Peterking to his Dudley congregation to be sincere Christians and not to indulge in vices, which could adversely affect their eternal destiny. Note the repetition of 'blame' and 'so sad'.

Pastor Peterking	Sometimes we get weak. What do we do? **Blame** others.
Congregational response	**Blame** yourself, Yes.
Pastor Peterking	It will be a sad cry for the drunkard and the smoker this morning that is in the street.
Congregational response	Hmhmh, yes, preach it sir.
Pastor Peterking	Both of us to meet up at the same place
Congregational response	My God, my God.
Pastor Peterking	It will be **so sad.**
Congregational response	**So sad**, so sad.

The first-generation preachers often made direct reference to heaven and hell and eschatological themes. The songs and choruses reflect themes of heaven and these ministers would sometimes state or sing repeatedly segments of songs in the middle or at the end of sermons to illustrate that theme. For example as the songwriter said: 'When we get to heaven at the marriage supper, all the saints will gather at the last assembling.'

Preachers often explicitly instruct the congregation to repeat the exact words uttered so as to engage them with the topic or a particular theme of the sermon. This request is referred to as the performer's cue, discussed in detail later in this chapter. Bishop John Francis offers this performance:

Bishop Francis (call)	Somebody holla fire
Congregation (response)	Fire
Bishop Francis	Somebody shout fire
Congregation (response)	Fire

Preachers also tell congregants to repeat words uttered from the pulpit to each other. Invariably, preachers employ the invocation 'Turn to your neighbour ...' or 'Tell your neighbour ...' Take the following example from the late Dr Wale Akinyemi preaching at a church in London:

Preacher (call)	How many people know we have the answer?
Congregation (response)	Amen, oh yes.
Preacher (call) (he laughs)	Tell your neighbour, say, 'you have the answer.'
Congregation (response)	You have the answer.

Bishop John Francis frequently employs this strategy. To affirm his points, he often says. 'Look at someone and say ...'. Take the following example from the bishop and also note the repetition of the key phrase, 'wake it up'.

Bishop Francis (call)	Look at someone and say, 'wake it up, wake it up, wake it up, wake it up, wake it up.'
Congregation (response)	Wake it up, wake it up, wake it up.
Bishop Francis (call)	God told me to tell you to wake up the Word.

Note the metaphor and imagery of the repetitious creole phrasing in 'wake it up' and 'wake up the Word'. The audience understands that wake up the Word means to make the Word, that is the Bible, come alive through adhering to its tenets. The apostle James in James 1.22 states: 'But be doers of the word, and not hearers only, deceiving yourselves' (NKJV). The bishop could have simply read from the biblical text to present his ideas, but metaphors and image-making, as previously discussed, form a critical part of preaching and aids in eliciting responses.

Often, repetitious phrases add to the sound and motion element in black Pentecostal churches, discussed in Chapter 2, suggesting the African ontology of a spiritual world composed of interactive forces (Sutcliffe and Tomlin 1986). Prophetess Tamika Pusey-Squire from Restoration Fellowship Ministries, Birmingham and her congregants are engaged in a marked sequential call–response repetitious dialogue through the use of sound and motion:

Prophetess Tamika (call)	I want you to say out loud with me 'This is my transitioning season.'
Congregation (response)	This is my transitioning season.
Prophetess Tamika (call)	Say it again.
Congregation (response)	This is my transitioning season.
Prophetess Tamika (call)	Listen to me I want you to say this as well: 'The person you see today is not the person you see tomorrow.'
Congregation (response)	The person you see today is not the person you see tomorrow.

During this repetitious dialogue, the prophetess stamps her feet by jumping up and down and the congregants are on their feet clapping and responding appropriately.

Tracking

I extend on Smitherman's description of repetition by outlining a device which I refer to as 'tracking'. This is where the preacher asks an individual to read a verse or passage from the Bible. The preacher then stops the reader after each sentence from the biblical text and in turn repeats the words of the reader; the minister then explicates the text either after each pause or in a call–response sequential reading. Prophetess Juanita Bynum often uses this device, when she requests Tashawn, her pastoral assistant, to read a particular passage of the Bible. (A pastoral assistant is known as an 'armour bearer' in some Pentecostal churches globally especially in North America, and in some BMCs in Britain.) Note the following example and also the prophetess's 'anhah' to each time Tashawn reads a verse:

Juanita	Read what it says (Isaiah 48.1)
Tashawn	Hear this oh House of Jacob
Juanita	anhah
Tashawn	and who come forth from the seed of Jacob
Juanita	anhahn, came out of praise, go ahead.
Tashawn	You who swear allegiance

Juanita	anhah
Tashawn	by the name of the Lord
Juanita	anhah
Tashawn	and make mention of the God of Israel
Juanita	anhah
Tashawn	but not in truth and sincerity
Juanita	(stressed) but not in truth and sincerity. You who make mention of God and swear allegiance but not with truth and sincerity. Read the Bible
Tashawn	nor in righteousness
Juanita	wait, wait, wait, he's saying here not in righteousness, so what God is trying to establish here is there is another level of living righteously that he desires for us to go into.
Congregation	Hallelujah, praise the Lord.
Juanita	When I say another level, let me clarify that ...

It is highly probable that tracking developed during the slavery era when slaves were forbidden to read and write, yet this device continues today in some Pentecostal churches in the diaspora, even in churches where congregants are highly literate. It could also underpin the ACS where the whole group are involved in the communication process. In many contemporary churches songs and choruses are often visually projected. However, throughout Pentecostal churches in the African diaspora one can still be requested to 'track out' a song where the tune or melody is known but the lyrics are unfamiliar to congregants. When this method is utilized in singing, the lead singer 'tracks' or says the words of each line of a song. The audience or congregation repeats the lines by singing them. Tracking is also used in small prayer, Bible or house group meetings where an individual may feel 'led by the Spirit' to raise (sing) a song that may not be well known to most people in the group. Tracking is sometimes used in my own church on occasions when a song is unfamiliar to many of the congregants.

Completer statements

Unlike tracking, completer statements depend on a high level of familiarity. Smitherman identifies this type of response as comments that complete the statement of the main speaker. Sometimes they occur in response to a request from the speaker; sometimes they occur spontaneously. This is a particularly common strategy in the sacred realm. Often preachers use well-known songs, choruses and biblical verses that form a valuable knowledge base which can be drawn upon through call–response behaviour. Preachers will often say 'and the Word says …' and the congregation is expected to complete the verse or will deliberately pause for a couple of seconds at key points in a sentence for the audience to complete the statement. Take the following example where Pastor Peterking makes reference to the omnipotence of God by using the words of a familiar chorus:

Pastor Peterking (call)	But don't God know us?
Congregation (response)	Yes, Sar Yes.
Pastor Peterking (call)	What do we sing sometimes? 'Whether we are wrong …
Congregation (response)	'or whether we are right, He knows.'

The group usually responds in unison and both the speaker and audience are a part of one organic whole. It illustrates group solidarity and the communal aspects of the African worldview.

In the example below the sequence is much more instructive when Prophetess Tamika asks the congregants to complete the word by leaving it in mid-air for them to complete:

Prophetess Tamika (call)	I want you to say it again with conviction: 'God is moving me forward'
Prophetess Tamika (call)	God is moving me …
Congregation (response)	forward
Prophetess Tamika (call)	God is moving me …

Congregation (response)	(louder) forward
Prophetess Tamika (call)	God is moving me …
Congregation (response)	(louder still) forward.

The performer's cues

The audience often responds spontaneously to the preacher's call. However, there are occasions when the preacher will give directives and specifically make a request for the audience to respond as in the following instance by Prophetess Tamika Pusey-Squire:

Prophetess Tamika (call)	Amen, Amen, Praise the Lord, Hallelujah Jesus, Glory to God. Can we just give God some praise …
Congregation (response)	Glory, Yes, Hallelujah, Praise Him, Praise Him (hand clapping).

In this way congregants are invited to become active participants and phrases such as 'Can we just give God some praise' are used to implore congregants to enter into worship as a prelude to the preaching event. There is a releasing of energies through sound and motion and the performer's cue is often used to 'set the atmosphere' which enables the preacher to present their homily with additional confidence, freely and with a great deal of dynamism.

The calls that are used in this way are well known. In several African cultures, for instance, the permission of the audience to begin a narrative performance is invoked by the use of a set formula such as the following Hausa example (Dalphinis, 1985, p. 182):

Narrator (call)	Gata nan gata nan ku (Here's a story for you)
Audience (response)	Ta so mu ju ta (It come we hear it – let us hear it)

In most other contexts the calls employed by performers are invariably in the form of a question to which the audience respond. For example, Blues singers often state: 'Will somebody help me?' at the end of a musical phrase, or Hip Hop artists will shout: 'Is there anybody in the house?' Or 'Give X a shout out.' In the sacred realm, people who testify invoke the formula 'Shall we praise the Lord', while preachers intersperse their sermons with a variety of phrases. For example, 'Can I have a witness?' (This is an African American phrase meaning, 'Can someone validate what I am saying'?) Or 'Let the Church say amen', 'Will somebody help me?' or 'Hello?' These are phrases used by ministers in Africa and throughout the diaspora to signal their calls for a response. By the same token a person who offers a testimony will begin with 'Shall we praise the Lord?' As Rickford and Rickford (2000, p. 51) explain:

> Black preachers demand participation from their congregations. If they so much sense a lull, they will not hesitate to ask ... 'How much time I got left!' to which the only proper response is: 'Take your time, Preach!' Preachers also use a range of non-verbal signals to elicit a response from the audience. For instance, they sometimes jump up and down or hit the pulpit.

Overlapping

The discussion has so far focused on the range of devices used by the performer to cue the audience response. Sometimes there is a smooth transition from call to response and on most occasions, there is a high degree of overlapping. Various writers discuss this phenomenon in diasporan communities. For example, Reisman (1974), as discussed in Chapter 5, refers to this highly interactive style where voices speak at the same time as contrapuntal. According to Rosenberg (1988), the antiphonal nature of sermons invites audience participation. Take the following example from Pastor Jackson at the New Testament Church of God in Dudley:

Pastor Jackson (call)	Woe unto them that] ...
Congregation (overlapping response)	(That stay at ease in Zion).

Thus in this case, the Bible or the 'word' then becomes an essential aspect of the discourse and informs the theology and verbal repertoire.

Tonal semantics in call–response

There are other situations where the performer uses a range of other devices that elicit responses, such as tonal semantics. Although this strategy is used in call–response behaviours it has been explored in the previous chapter as a separate category of this Pentecostal style of preaching. The use of the voice to create rhythm is key to tonal semantics. Take the following extract from a powerful sermon entitled: *God is a Jealous God* delivered by Pastor Ulrich Rolle, from Antigua.

Pastor Rolle	He is saying you ought to be mine. You ought to be mine exclusively.
Congregational response	Amen, praise the Lord.
Pastor Rolle	You see when God separates a nation or life unto Himself. It ought to be mine and nobody else. It ought to be mine wholly. It ought to be mine truly. It ought to be mine completely because I am a jealous God.

Pastor Rolle places exaggerated stress at regular intervals throughout the first call and the words, which follow in the second call. The exaggerated stress, in combination with the loud delivery, ensures that the congregation become emotionally involved in the sermon. In this excerpt note the use of words such as 'Himself', 'else', 'wholly', 'truly' and 'completely' to create rhythm and cadence. Note also the repetition of 'It ought to be mine', which further enhances the rhythm.

Preachers often use deliberately slow and exaggerated pronunciation of important words. Rather than say 'God', for instance, they will pronounce it as Godt and aspirate on the final consonant. In the extract above, the climax is punctuated by dramatic inhalations that can be described as intoned groans, which is an African retention.

In addition, preachers frequently make use of elongated articulation of single words, heavy breathing and extremely rapid speech or heavy pauses. 'Talk-singing' of this kind often signals the climax of the sermon and arouses appropriate responses from the congregation. Take the following example from Bishop T. D. Jakes:

T. D. Jakes	You've got to press till something breaks You've got to press till something moves You don't get there if you don't press Nothing happens if you don't press You've got to press, press, My God My God My God.
Congregational response	Praise the Lord, Praise Jesus, Glory.

Note the emphasis and also repetition of the phases 'You've got to press', 'if you don't press' and the actual word 'press'. The rhythmic qualities of words often make this type of preaching distinctive. Sometimes the delivery can be slow and deliberate, making use of JC as in the Jamaican or British context. The playing of a musical instrument, invariably a keyboard, usually accompanies the delivery of tonal semantics. Note the example below of an extract from a sermon by Pastor Peterking who ironically is talking about music and two famous pop stars:

Pastor Peterking	Bob Marley he get shot down by a mad gun man (Bob Marley got shot down by a mad man who had a gun)
Congregational response	My God, my God, hmhm.

Pastor Peterking	Elvis Presley, the man tun fat and bloated (The man became fat and bloated) He played in church but the church was too Slowww (elongated) (He played in church but it was far too slow for him)
Pastor Peterking	But a thing done slowly is done
Congregation (overlapping response)	is done surely. is done surely. (Jamaican proverbial expression meaning that something carried out at a slow pace is often executed well.)

Each sentence is enmeshed with JC, and a proverbial expression is inserted, 'But a thing done slowly is done surely', to make the point forcefully, and the congregation aware of this proverb also anticipates and completes the statement and their voices overlap. As previously discussed proverbs in diasporan communities form an important part of an inherited oral tradition and are widely used in African cultures (Watson, 1991). Very often, themes concerning the raging battle between good and evil and the satanic influences that pervade the world are emphasized explicitly by preachers. Pastor Peterking's delivery also illustrates the clear distinction black Pentecostals make about participating in what is considered 'worldly' activities, such as secular music, that could adversely affect one's spirituality, as discussed in Chapter 4. The reference to two well-known singers: Bob Marley and Elvis Presley who both experienced an unfortunate fate, and the use of the tonal phrase 'The church was too sloww' are intended to demonstrate that Christians should be aware of the dangers in living precariously. As church members are strongly advised and admonished to remain untainted from the 'world' or social entertainment such as 'clubbing', this extract fits into the Pentecostal theology inherent in these churches. Having said this, in

America there appears to be a disjuncture or 'crossing over' within the sacred–secular realm of the music industry, which is widely debated, but there remains a core of gospel singers and musicians who are 'strictly gospel'. However, in Britain, gospel singing artistes tend to perform primarily within the sacred sphere, but there is border crossing among gospel musicians.

Another feature of call–response that does not appear to be documented in the homiletic literature is the use of handkerchiefs. The audience sometimes wave handkerchiefs in symphony and often to music at intense moments, in response to the calls from the performer or the preacher. Preachers will also sometimes wave their handkerchief almost as an invocation for the audience to enter into the spirit of worship.

Summary

Call–response, then, is the African communication process whereby the audience either repeats or adds to the performer's (preacher's) statements. It takes a variety of forms including co-signing, On-T, encouraging, repetition and completer statements. These categories form a useful framework for discussion. Nevertheless, they should not be viewed as totally discrete, as there is some degree of amalgamation between them. Call–response is also reflected in the performer's cue, and preachers often make use of shared knowledge to cue congregants. In these instances, tonal semantics or distinctive prosody is used as prompts for responses. Pentecostals also utilize call–response in a device referred to as 'tracking'. In addition to the more structured call–response elements there is also a great deal of overlapping between speakers. The level of cooperation and the shared responsibility for preaching is underpinned by a shared core theological knowledge. All the components of call–response are of course common throughout the diaspora in speech and music and in both sacred and secular contexts. Call–response is a core feature of African Caribbean Pentecostal preaching that gives credence to the resonance of African oral culture in diverse geographical sacred spaces such as Britain.

Reflection and activities

The stylistic features of this type of Pentecostal preaching depend on the African communication technique of call–response. List the ways that you can elicit responses from congregants that are culturally familiar to your setting.

Read the following:

While call–response lends itself to audience participation, the preacher is still the central figure and perceived as an authoritative bearer of biblical knowledge and insight. The listening audience are not invited to make specific comments during the preaching event. Even in Pentecostal spaces such as those described in this book, where congregants are active listeners, they are still the recipients of knowledge. I and fellow ministers in my local church have adopted the ideas below to facilitate preaching that is more dialogic, whereby congregants are invited to comment or respond to the content or theme of the sermon. In this way they are co-constructors of the preaching act. In this sense it takes a broader view of call–response as a communicative device and obviously entails improvisation. The co-construction of preaching is not a common occurrence for a Sunday worship service in any Christian tradition and it is recommended that this approach be carried out only periodically. This approach can yield immense satisfaction for both clergy and laity and it is certainly worth attempting.

- You may consider introducing your sermon by asking a series of general questions related to the main theme of the sermon. You may need to inform the congregants of your intentions at the beginning of the sermon.
- You may also conclude the sermon by asking congregants to respond to any of the ideas that you have presented.
- Depending on the size of your congregation, you may wish to request that individuals work in pairs to respond to a couple of key questions. You may also decide to have feedback.

7

Restating the Claim: Repetition in Preaching

The discussion of call–response in preaching inevitably entailed some reference to the significance of repetition that is not restricted to call–response behaviour. It is a phenomenon that permeates several kinds of speech events in diasporic communities and repetition can vary in length from single words to much lengthier units such as the refrains of epics. Repetition is an extremely critical component of Pentecostal preaching. This chapter will look at the different forms of repetition and the various functions it serves.

In some societies, specific words and phrases tend to be repeated for a limited and designed effect. The use of repetition as a stylistic device appears to be far more widespread in societies that are orally inclined. The meaning attached to repetition in oral and literate contexts is also very different. Edwards and Sienkewicz (1990, p. 144) confirm this point by comparing the sonnet with a sermon by a black preacher:

> In the sonnet, nothing can be redundant or aggregate. In the sermon and other forms of oral art, repeatable forms like formulae ... are an essential part of the communal basket of threads from which the performance is woven. Thus the structural unity of the written word is analytic and creates unity by trimming the excess and the irrelevant, while in the oral world structural unity is essentially synthetic, a constant elaboration of elements added to the fibre of the web of words.

The ways preachers use repetition to present biblical texts is an important stylistic device. The focus on repetition as a part of the ACS is subsumed in other kinds of discourses in diasporic communities, taking a variety of forms including reduplication, simple repetition, near repetition and lists that serve many functions. In addition, the dramatic and crescendo effect is reliant on repetitive structures, critical to the preacher's verbal framework. Let us now turn to the forms of repetition.

Reduplication

Reduplication is a feature of many West African languages, which has attracted frequent commentary (see Bailey 1966; Todd 1984). It is a productive process in language, whereby words are repeated to form a compound with a variety of meanings. In JC for example, it can be used for emphasis, as in 'no-no' (definitely not); continual habitual action as in 'cry-cry' (always crying); abundance as in 'huoli-huoli' (having many holes or in the sacred domain, sanctimonious); alliteration as in 'knock-knock' (to keep on knocking); attribution as in 'redi-redi' (reddish); distribution as in 'little-little' (a little here and a little there); and for plural reference as in 'was-was' (wasps).

Take the extract of the sermon: 'Elevated by the Power of God' by Pastor Nathan. He uses reduplication in the phrases 'come-come, come-come, come-come' when referring to how the moderator has to cajole congregants into worship. The phrase 'come-come' means 'come on'. Reduplication involves the formation of compound verbs, nouns or adjectives.

Simple repetition

Another feature of repetition is what we might label as 'simple repetition', the repetition of a single word, a phrase or even an entire sentence to achieve varied effects. It is a common feature of black Pentecostal preaching. Take the following example from a preacher in London:

Jesus is Wonderful.
Jesus is Wonderful.
Jesus is Wonderful.

In the 'I Have a Dream' speech by Dr Martin Luther King, the phrase 'I have a dream' is repeated at least seven times in one segment of the speech. Similarly, Pastor Peterking repeated the title of his sermon, 'The Counsel of the Lord That Shall Stand', a number of times throughout his homily. Pastor Penny Francis, co-pastor of Ruach, uses repetition in an outstanding sermon she delivered entitled, 'He tricked me in the wilderness'. Notably, each time a word or phrase is repeated there is a short pause for special effect. Repetition in preaching aids memory and it draws attention to important biblical themes and reinforces biblical principles (see Tomlin 1999).

The most dramatic use of the simple repetition of a single word is to be found in music. Take for instance the word 'Jesus' in the gospel chorus of the same name. The refrain consists quite simply of:

Jesus, Jesus
Jesus, Jesus ...

Simple repetition of an entire sentence is also a common feature of a variety of genres. Take the famous song: 'No Woman No Cry' by the late Jamaican reggae artist Bob Marley. The song centres on the challenges experienced by a woman who is exhorted not to cry:

Lead	No woman no cry
Background	No woman no cry
Lead	No woman no cry
Background	No woman no cry

It should be pointed out that simple repetition is seldom restricted to words or phrases or sentences. Most often, different layers of repetition are woven into the performance as in the case of the chorus below.

Cast your burdens unto Jesus for he cares for you,
Cast your burdens unto Jesus for he cares for you.
Higher, higher, higher, higher, higher, higher, higher, higher,
Lift Jesus higher,
Lower, lower, lower, lower, lower, lower, lower, lower, lower,
Stamp satan lower.

In this example there is the repetition of single words like 'higher' and 'lower' and whole sentences as in 'Cast your burdens unto Jesus for he cares for you.'

Near repetition

Closely related to simple repetition is a stylistic device labelled 'elegant variation' by Callendar and Cameron (1990, p. 19). In this case we are dealing with a near repetition or paraphrase. Speakers or performers often use elegant variation to acknowledge the presence of the audience by paying a courteous salute. In the sacred contexts speakers will often prefix their exegesis with 'Greetings to my pastor, greetings to the saints and visiting friends.' This type of repetition is also illustrated in the following sermon extract:

Do you know Jesus?
Do you know Jesus?
Do you know he lifted me up from the miry clay?
He lifted me and put me on the rock to stay.
King of Kings and Lord of Lords
Worship him today
Worship him for he is the King and Lord

Here we see the alternation of elegant variation between 'Jesus' and 'he lifted me up' and 'worship' and 'King' and 'Lord'.

Lists

Lists are repetitive structures, which allow the speaker to develop a point. This deals with not the same word but the same grammatical structures. Take for instance, the list of God's attributes outlined in a sermon by Minister Abegail from Restoration Fellowship Ministries:

> The Lord is good
> The Lord is great
> He is awesome
> Jesus is the Lord and we cannot do without him.

Similarly, Bishop Louis Mcleod from the New Testament Church of God in Lee, London:

> God told me to tell the church to get in line
> If you want power get in line
> If you want healing get in line
> If you want prophecy get in line
> Anything you want get in line with God and He will do something.

Lists are often used as a signal for audience response. In a mainstream British context, the competent orator will indicate appropriate points for audience response by using such rhetorical devices as three-part lists (Callender and Cameron 1990). It is interesting to note, however, that lists are used differently in black speech events. Here, listeners do not wait for the completion of a list before making their response. Take this extract from Pastor Esther where the listing focuses on the character of God with the repeated phrase, 'those of you who think/ those of you that think':

Pastor Esther	So I want to talk about the patience God has for us. Are you ready for the scriptures guys? Second Peter three verse eight

[2 Peter 3.8] says: 'But beloved do not forget this one thing, that with the Lord one day is as a thousand years, and a thousand years as one day.' So for those of you who think God you are taking too long, one day is a thousand years.

Congregational response Praise God, Amen.

Pastor Esther I think we can wait two or three more days for God to answer. Those of you that think that God is slack, slackness does not define who God is, that is not his character and not his nature so we need to repent.

Congregational response Amen, woi, oh yes.

Pastor Esther And those of you that think God you know what I've suffered too long. He's actually saying that I'm suffering for too long waiting for you to come to the knowledge of who you are and who I am. It says in second Corinthians five verse nineteen [2 Corinthians 5.19] 'that God was in Christ reconciling the world to Himself, not imputing their trespasses to them, and has committed to us the word of reconciliation'. So those people who you think you're out of relationship with, you need to reconcile because the Christian message is re-concilia-tion if they choose not to accept you, dust your feet it's a boundary and keep it moving in love.

Congregational response Amen, my Lord.

Functions of repetition

Repetition has several functions in preaching and has already been hinted at in the discussion of the different forms that it can take. Here we focus on the ways in which repetition provides scaffolding for both preachers and congregants, by emphasizing shared biblical themes and values. Repetition can be used as an important aid to learning and calls attention to important themes. It helps the audience to memorize the preacher's message. It also contributes to the dramatic effect or adds humour to the homily. Significantly, repetition has an interactional function. Repeating the words, phrases or sentences of others shows responsiveness and support. In the context of preaching, shared meanings and shared assumptions help to consolidate the bonds between the preacher and congregants, uniting them in a single purpose, that is the fight between good and evil. Both entities are a part of one organic whole. Like the call–response elements, repetition clearly demonstrates underlying aspects of the traditional African worldview by pointing to the communal outlook of life.

In addition, repetition allows speakers to think what they are going to say next, a process first described by Parry (1930) as 'composition in performance'. The various different forms of repetition described above provide both the structure and building blocks for speech. With these foundations preachers are able to improvise and combine different elements in innovative and creative ways.

Formulae as a rhetorical strategy

The idea of the formula is often invoked in discussion of composition in performance (Finnegan 2012). By being able to resort to many well-known words, phrases and sentences, the performer has time to think ahead. Formulae are used in a wide variety of contexts in African and diasporic communities and the sacred setting is no exception. The formula is used in testimonies, which provide opportunities for members to report on God's goodness and their own spiritual experiences or encounters. Testimonies follow a particular format, especially with older members and in rather traditional churches, as previously mentioned, referencing churches with a higher degree of Caribbean influences in the liturgy. Usually the person who testifies begins with 'Shall we praise the Lord?' (In Oneness churches it also begins with 'Praise the Lord saints'). This formula may be repeated several times as the spiritual tempo increases.

Testifier (call)	Shall we praise the Lord?
Congregation (response)	Praise the Lord
Testifier (call)	Shall we praise the Lord again?
Congregation (response)	Praise the Lord
Testifier (call)	(louder) Shall we praise the Lord again?

Older members would continue the introduction by extending greetings to the main ministry team. For example:

> 'Greetings to pastor X, deacons, brothers and sisters.'

Other formulas include:

> 'Greetings in the name of Jesus our soon coming King.'

Often, the testifier sometimes uses the formula: 'As the songwriter says ...' For instance:

> As the songwriter says:
> 'I love the Lord deep down in my heart
> Not an earthly vein can cause me to depart.'

Guest preachers are also expected to extend due respect to God and to all the other dignitaries that are seated on the platform or at the front of the church. According to Mitchell (1990), these formulaic greetings resemble the praise speeches reported in West African culture.

Prayers often draw on formulas. Below is a recording of a prayer by Sister Hyacinth Comrie from Leeds, given for me!

Oh God, I put your daughter before thee,
Oh God, you have given her a word that passeth all understanding,
And I am asking you Oh God as she speaks your word that fire will come upon her, Father,
And whoever she speaks to Father God, whoever she ministers to Father God, your presence will shine Father God,
Healing is her portion,
Her feet Father God. Her feet as she takes your word, we pray that the anointing will be upon her and around her, in the name of Yeshua.
Lord let your will be done in the life of your daughter.
Let your will be done in heaven and on earth.
Lord God she's here for a reason and for a purpose.
You've called her, you've anointed her, you've appointed her for such a time as this,
so Father God cover her with your choicest blessings and cover her with your blood, the blood that passeth all understanding.
Father God we call upon the angels to surround her, in the name of Yeshua.
Lord Jesus Adonai, we call upon you in the name of Jesus right now.
Father God draw your sword as she covers herself with the whole armour of God,
and Father God to withstand the wiles of the enemy.
We pray Father God that the work will be done, Father.
So Father we say thank you. I say thank you for your daughter.
Thank you for her ministry. Thank you for the ministry Father God.
It's not just in this church, Father God it's world wide.
So thank you for the ministry, in the name of Yeshua
We say thank you in Jesus name.

The formulaic vocatives 'Oh God' and 'Father God' appear repeatedly throughout the prayer and give the composer the necessary time to consider what to say next. Old English phrases of 'thee' and 'passeth' are also obvious, which typify compositions of prayers especially of the first-generation Caribbean denoting engagement with the King James' version of the Bible. (See also Finnegan 2012 for a discussion on the use of formulas in African prayers.)

Speaking of the use of oral formulas in preaching, LaRue (2011, Appendix A) lists,

> clichés, colloquial expressions, adages, aphorisms, maxims, and mottos. They can also be made up of well-known hymns, poems, and other expressions that signify ... Many sermons are peppered with them, and the black congregation usually immediately understand the sense in which they are being employed.

Erickson (1984, pp. 93–4) explains the strategies employed in speech among people in the diaspora by referring to the classical Greek oral tradition, described by Aristotle. The term 'prosographia', used by Aristotle, describes commonplace topics or themes that have clusters of related details. Erickson believes that the purpose of the speaker is to persuade and arouse the emotions of the audience by means of a commonplace theme. In many African oral narratives, for example, certain phrases, lines and even the whole framework of details are used repeatedly for constructing successive stages in the story (Okpewho 1992). In the same way, by relying on the familiar the preacher can think ahead. The congregants for their part are given a framework in which familiarity is an important scaffold for memorability.

The context of African Caribbean preaching like other speech events is fixed with specific structures, which provide a baseline for composition. The rigid order of the service, as discussed in Chapter 2, is in marked contrast with the degree of extemporization that takes place. Holt (1972, p.191) states that the black church 'has a ritual nearly as rigid and unvarying as that used by the Catholic and High Lutheran services'. Sermons also draw on repeated phrases as can be seen in the example of Pastor Esther above. It is interesting to note that while the overall structure for the service is invariable this very stability serves as a prop for composition of the sermon.

The dramatic and crescendo effect

Repetition has its own aesthetic. It is not a tool simply to help the preacher to think on their feet, nor for imprinting a message in the minds of the audience. It is a powerful stylistic device for the preacher who wishes to create dramatic effect, also known as dramatic repetition. Each repetition is often accompanied by a crescendo, leading to a climax, which allows the preacher to hold the floor, to sway the audience, to stir the emotions or make a point.

Prosodic features or the tonal semantics already described in Chapters 5 and 6, including pitch, stress and tone, also play a critical part in creating the dramatic effect associated with repetition. The dramatic effect that leads to a climax is apparent in a wide variety of speech event such as gospel singing, especially live performances, and are particularly evident in preaching. Take the following example that can be found in any African Caribbean church in Britain and notice the responses of the congregations, which grows progressively louder until they reach a dramatic climax.

Pastor (quiet)	Let's praise the Lord
Congregation	Praise the Lord
Pastor (slightly louder)	Let's praise the Lord again
Congregation (slightly louder)	Praise the Lord
Pastor (even louder)	I can't hear you. Praise the Lord
Congregation (very loud)	Praise the Lord
Pastor (very loud)	Come on, let's praise the Lord
Congregation (very loud indeed)	Praise the Lord
Pastor (very loud indeed)	Praise him again

Both the preacher and congregants are involved in repetitious dialogue and the phrase 'Praise the Lord' could continue for much longer than recorded here. Intonation, stress, tone of voice and other paralinguistic signals all contribute to a powerful and unmistakable crescendo. Rosenberg (1988) opines that repetition adds to the increasing emotional intensity and of course contributes to the sound and motion element. The extract below, by Pastor Esther, is a much more descriptive example of the crescendo effect.

Pastor Esther	Psalm a hundred and three verse eight [Ps. 103.8] says 'The Lord *is* merciful and gracious, Slow to anger, and abounding in mercy.'
Pastor Esther (moderate tone)	**You wanna be like Christ?** You need to be merciful, gracious, slow to anger, abounding in compassion and showing loving kindness. Exodus thirty-four verse six (Exodus 34.6), 'Then Lord passed before Him, [Moses] and proclaimed, "The Lord, the Lord God, merciful and gracious, longsuffering, and abounding in goodness and truth."'
Pastor Esther (moderate tone)	**You wanna be like Jesus?** You need to have compassion, be gracious, slow to anger, abounding in loving kindness, truth and faithfulness.
Congregational response	Come on, come on, come on ...
Pastor Esther	Psalm a hundred and forty-five verse eight [Ps. 145.8] says 'The Lord *is* gracious and full of compassion, Slow to anger and great in mercy.'

Pastor Esther (louder)	**You wanna be like Jesus?** You need to be full of compassion, slow to anger, abounding in loving kindness. Psalm eighty-six verse fifteen [Ps. 86.15] 'But You O Lord, *are* a God full of compassion, and gracious, longsuffering and abundant in mercy and truth.'
Pastor Esther (even louder)	**You wanna be like Jesus?**
Congregational response	Amen, Amen, Amen.
Pastor Esther:	You need to be merciful, gracious, slow to anger, abounding in loving kindness and walking in truth. Joel two verse thirteen [Joel 2.13] 'So rend your heart, and not your garments; Return to the Lord your God, For He *is* gracious and merciful, Slow to anger, and of great kindness; And He relents from doing harm.' Rip your hearts into pieces.
Pastor Esther (very loud)	**You wanna be like Jesus?** You need to have grace, you need to render your heart and not your garment, you need to have compassion, you need to be slow in anger, abounding in loving kindness, faithful to his covenant and his people and also sentence other people's evil when they genuinely repent to you …
Congregational response	That's right Jesus, yes.
Pastor Esther	Acts thirteen verse eighteen [Acts 13.18] 'Now for a time of about forty years He put up with their ways in the wilderness.'

(Very loud)	**You wanna be like Jesus?** Put up with their behaviour in the wilderness.
Congregational response	Wow, wow.
Pastor Esther	Isaiah forty-eight verse 9 [Isa. 48.9] 'For My name's sake I will defer My anger.'
Pastor Esther **(louder still)**	**You wanna be like Jesus?** Stop cutting people off. Restrain yourself, refrain from wrath and you have the mind of Jesus [1 Corinthians 2.16]. Nehemiah nine verse seventeen (Neh. 9.17) But you *are* God, Ready to pardon, Gracious and merciful, Slow to anger, Abundant in kindness, And did not forsake them' … gracious, merciful compassionate …
Congregational response	Glory, my God, my God, my God, Jesus. (Individuals stand up and raise right hand and point to the preacher signalling agreement)
Pastor Esther **(very loud indeed)**	**You wanna be like Jesus?** Stop abandoning people, be slow in anger, abounding in loving kindness, be compassionate when they don't listen to your advice and they keep going off and when they get their necks stiff give you that facety (JC) [feisty] look, love them and walk through it because **you want to be like Jesus.** I think I have made the point …
Congregational response	Laughter.

In this sermon the phrase 'You wanna be like Jesus?' is repeated several times for both clarity and stress. The cadence of her delivery is captivating and the repetitious tonal phrasing emphasizes the rhetorical question, 'You wanna be like Jesus?' that increases in volume with each segment. The call–response aspects of this example have, of course, been developed in greater detail in Chapter 6. Humour is injected at the end of this excerpt with the phrase 'I think I have made the point'.

In terms of humour, repetition adds to its effect in preaching. The following extract from Pastor Peterking illustrates the humorous use of repetition. The pastor is making a play on the contrast between physical and spiritual beauty

Pastor Peterking	I have two sisters. One said she wanted to marry a pretty man and she did marry a *pretty man* (pause) him ugly ...
Congregation	(roars with laughter]
Pastor Peterking	My other sister, she marry a man who wasn't an oil painting, if you know what I mean
Congregation	(laughter)
Pastor Peterking	But the man's ways was so *pretty*.

Pastor Peterking chose a word, which Reisman (1974) describes as 'free flowing' and which allows the audience to interpret the meaning in their own way. The use of 'pretty' to describe a man is in itself amusing. Each repetition of pretty heightens the humour. The juxtaposition of pretty and ugly adds further to this effect. Note too Pastor Peterking's delivery of the punchline in each comment marked by distinctive creole intonation and in the first instance also by creole syntax. This has the effect of bonding the pastor and the congregation and further underlies shared experiences and expectations.

Summary

In examining the range of forms which repetition takes, it is possible to make two main observations. First, repetition is expressed in different ways: from reduplication to the lists. We have mainly touched upon those that are particularly relevant for African Caribbean Pentecostal preaching. Second, these different forms are combined in several ways. Rather than viewing repetition as tedious, a closer analysis reveals how different kinds of repetition are skilfully interlocked to fulfil a number of functions and to achieve a range of stylistic effects. It allows the preacher to think on their feet. It provides the framework and stability for enormous creativity. It helps congregants to be involved. It supports shared biblical values. It also creates humour. Finally, it is a means of creating dramatic effect. By combining repetition with crescendo, the preacher can hold attention, inspire and excite, and amuse while communicating biblical truths.

Reflection and activities

- Why might the use of repetition be considered as 'tedious'?
- In your opinion, which of the repetitious devices identified above would you consider superfluous or redundant for your particular cultural context? Why might this be so?
- Focus on a sermon that you are preparing presently. Can you suggest where 'near repetition' could be utilized in the main body of the homily?
- Focus on any of the sermonic excerpts based on the stylistic device of repetition in this chapter. Which one(s) do you find most appealing? Think of at least two reasons to support your response.

8

Conclusion

> Christian faith must go on being translated, must continuously enter into the vernacular culture and interact with it, or it withers and fades. (Walls, 2002, p. 29)

Throughout this book I have analysed African Caribbean preaching in Pentecostal spaces in Britain. The underlying view has been that elements of African retentions are reflected in the homiletic practices of the clergy. At the beginning of the book we traced the history of black people in the diaspora to Africa and argued that although African slaves came in the main from West Africa, which had different languages and cultural practices, there were underlying similarities in the African ontology or worldview. The African ways of thinking, behaving and speaking appear to have been most preserved in the religious practices of the slaves and the oral manifestations of their spirituality. The prominence of orality in the African context, discussed in terms of the oral–literate continuum, was applied to the preaching genre of African Caribbean Pentecostals.

A starting point for Chapter 1 was the historiography of Pentecostalism, particularly the origins of modern Pentecostalism emanating from North America and an exploration of its African roots. In this chapter, we discussed the critical role of Bishop William Joseph Seymour, the acknowledged leader of the Azusa Street revival in Los Angeles which began in 1906. Attention was focused on African retentions inherited by Seymour and his compatriots at Azusa Street by surmising the religious praxis found in the slave and post-slave community. Despite the racial and doctrinal disputes at Azusa Street, the early Pentecostals were instrumental in expanding Pentecostalism worldwide including the Caribbean, especially in Jamaica. After the Second World War, Pentecostalism in Jamaica became the fastest growing religious movement, a fusion of indigenous spiritual expressions such as Myal and Christianity.

Chapter 2 identified that the Jamaicans were in fact the largest Caribbean population of the first or Windrush generation that came to Britain during the post-war period as originators of Pentecostalism among the African Caribbean community. This chapter briefly charted the migration of the Windrush generation and the Pentecostal churches they established. It provided an overview of the various theologies and focused on the heterogenic but overarching theological hallmarks of these churches. Chapter 2 also outlined the liturgical practices of African Caribbean Pentecostalism, particularly in the realm of prayers and the worship patterns of singing, music, dancing and hand clapping, which serve as underlays for the preaching event. It concluded by describing the release of sound and motion components in worship and preaching, suggesting the African ontology of a spiritual universe of interactive forces.

It is pivotal to shed light on the spectrum of communicative patterns of the African Caribbean speech community to illuminate the preaching genre. The origins and nature of their linguistic heritage is complex and discussed in Chapter 3. The genesis of the language of Africans during the slavery era arose as a result of the interaction between different language groups with European slave masters, thus giving rise to a pidgin, a basic form of communication. Over time with the subsequent generations a creole developed expressing the full communicative needs of the speakers. Creoles are qualitatively different from SE in terms of lexis, phonology, syntax and semantics. Creoles are spoken widely in the Caribbean and other parts of the world. The Windrush generation including the clergy spoke Jamaican Creole (JC) popularly known as Patois. It was hypothesized that in their attempts to speak Standard English (SE) some first-generation interlocutors drew on the BBC Received Pronunciation (RP) of the 1950s, which sometimes led to hypercorrection. The second generation, especially in the West Midlands and those belonging to Pentecostal churches, developed their ability to code-switch from SE or the local varieties of English to JC and British black talk (BBT), described as the hybridity of language among second and third generations.

The hermeneutics of African Caribbean homiletics was examined in Chapter 4. It sourced the orality of Pentecostal preaching in general to the African Americans at Azusa Street establishing the oral structures of Pentecostal theology. Ten markers of African Caribbean homiletics were identified, such as the expressive and performative nature of preaching, preaching in context and attire as signifiers. The chapter examined the reticence regarding theological education historically among Pentecostals in general, which has influenced Pentecostal hermeneutics. It also discussed the influences of prosperity theology in African Caribbean preaching and argued that it is unlikely to have full sway within the British context.

We moved from the historical background of African Caribbean Pentecostalism to the development of the structural components of language, that is lexis, syntax, etc., and the homiletics of preaching to its distinct stylistic features. The stylistic examines the ways in which the different elements of the structural characteristics are combined to create varied effects and have been discussed in several chapters including 5, 6 and 7. In Chapter 5 the artistic oratory of sermons demonstrated further the pre-eminence of speech implicating the ontology of African linguistic cultures. The umbrella term 'black preaching' followed its usage in the literature, as its facets are not solely confined to the Pentecostal tradition but evident among clergy in other denominations. Nor is it necessarily a racial code for Pentecostal preaching and can be seen across the ethnic divide in North America though culturally ascribed. The reason for this phenomenon in the United States can be located to the similar styles in the 'folk sermons' of black and white evangelicals during the Great Awakening. Moreover, media access to preaching from around the globe is testament to the cross-cultural tones of preaching. Chapter 5 also elucidated that preparation and delivery of homilies are dependent on a number of stylistic characteristics such as improvisation, proverbial expression and the dramatic presentation of self.

The African linguistic features of call and response were discussed in Chapter 6. Call–response, that requires the audience to add or echo the words of the performer or preacher, can take a variety of forms including co-signing, on-T, encouraging, repetition and completer statements. It can also take the form of the performer's cue where the speaker specifically requests the audience's response. Sometimes intonation or 'tonal semantics' is implemented as a cue for audience response. The use of call–response influencing communication, both verbal and listening, reveal the symbiotic relationship between the preacher and congregants. There is considerable overlap between speakers reflecting shared biblical knowledge. The communal nature of preaching demonstrates the highly interactive style of speech and denotes shared theological insights and group solidarity.

Repetition is another recurrent characteristic of preaching, analysed in Chapter 7. It also takes a number of different forms, from reduplication and the simple repetition of single words or phrases to near repetition and lists. These different forms of repetition are intertwined in different stylistic ways. The chapter also drew attention to formulas as a rhetorical strategy, exploring how preachers construct sermons through formulaic strategies. Repetition has a number of functions. It enables preachers to improvise and provides a platform for creativity and audience participation in the preaching event. It helps cement shared theological views as well as creating crescendo leading to the dramatic climax.

The genius of black preaching lies in its simultaneous use of language. Undoubtedly, African Caribbean Pentecostal preachers have tremendous oratorical skills utilizing a range of rhetorical devices. However, analyses of sermonic texts in these Pentecostal spaces suggest that recognition of the wider socio-economic and political issues affecting African Caribbean people are largely conspicuous by their absence. Homilies do not overtly include themes championing the cause of their constituents. It can be argued that while preaching is dynamic and uplifting, its prophetic voice as a vehicle for liberation and transformation may not be apparent.

Exorcism and preaching

Beckford's (2013) innovative exorcism theory is appropriated here to partially explain why sermonic texts appear disengaged from liberating themes. He uses bewitchment and exorcism as metaphors for naming social realities in transformative ways. He focuses on African and colonial retentions, the ways in which African motifs were reconfigured in slavery and the continued effects of colonization on African Caribbean Pentecostalism in Britain. Beckford emphasizes missionary bewitchment as a form of debased Christian ideals on black Christians. He seeks in particular to expose how black Pentecostals imbibe missionary theology in their liturgy, doctrine and language and their collusion with the rationality of racial terror as a form of occult practices. His inversion of the popular African imagery of 'bewitchment' attempts to decolonize it by exposing Western Christianity as occultic and posits that bewitchment in the slave world was both physical and mystical violence; the idea of mystical violence relatable to cosmological conflict pervading human life and material objects. He argues that the Eurocentric missionary endeavours continue to enslave and oppress black people and impacts on their theology which needs to be exorcised. To understand the complex history of colonialism in Africa and America, Cannibalism and Zombism are employed in metaphoric ways as motifs of bewitchment themes, the former as a 'rapacious consumption' and the other as a mindless body experience. Of particular interest is the form of black zombification, described by Beckford as epistemic violence 'imposition of one way of doing things that belittles and deceives the other' (Beckford 2013, p. 43). A parallel is given between the Gerasene demoniac, Legion, cited in Mark 5.1–15, who manifested gross mental instability which ended with Jesus' intervention, and the zombie image, and the experience of psychological slavery. He further considers Jesus' ministry of healing from satanic oppression (Acts 10.38).

Adedibu (2012) draws attention to the Gerasene model used by Beckford and rightly applauds it for sensitizing us to the realities of recolonization of African and Caribbean people. As Adedibu articulates, the Gerasene demoniac ceased to be a product of his past and did not have a 'post-demoniac syndrome'. Furthermore, most people of the African diaspora in Britain have not defined the legitimacy and distinctiveness of their identity, in a similar way to writers such as Beckford through the approximation of their 'Britishness', Caribbean background and intellectuality. Other factors can also be inserted at this point, to extend on Adedibu's aforementioned views relating to Pentecostal ministers. First, some African Caribbean Pentecostal preachers, mainly male, may feel ill-equipped to tackle the challenges affecting the lives of people belonging to their community, due to their own lack of education or in some cases, ambivalence regarding their cultural identity. Second, unlike in the African American context, where there is a plethora of well-established historically black colleges and universities (HBCUs), that are magnets for intellectual and theological engagement with issues pertaining to black people, the opposite is true for African Caribbean Pentecostals in Britain.

According to Adedibu (2012, p. 117), Beckford's view of exorcism of the colonial influences 'might constitute a distinctive paradigm to black theology as most blacks have shown conditioned reflexes to mastery and superiority of Western Christianity'. Adedibu also observes the continued retention of colonialism on the theology of African and Caribbean people despite the demise of the slave trade, such as highly valuing Eurocentrism over Africanization. Critically, he observes the failure of black people to 'renew their minds' on their ecclesiology in the sphere of political and social injustice. I concur with the views of both Beckford and Adedibu, which have far-reaching implications for the preaching discourse.

Beckford rightly advocates a middle-ground hermeneutics. In this scheme biblical texts are interpreted through contemporary social and cultural thought or medical explanations, and exorcism is given new meaning contemporaneously, not a rejection of the miraculous dimension of exorcism but a reinterpretation of its core meaning having relevance for modern times. The supernatural is paramount to Pentecostal belief system and as Aldred (2005, 2010) points out, black Pentecostal churches are essentially bibliocentric hence any preaching model has to entail both these aspects. Pentecostal preachers not only require, as Adedibu so eloquently states, a 'renewed mind' on political and social injustice, but also exorcism to support the idealized state of the mind, free as much as possible from the demonic forces of colonialism. It can be argued that both the colonial successors and colonized descendants could well benefit from this kind of exorcism to be 'free at last'.

How can Pentecostal ministers and clergy in the wider ecclesia put into practice Jesus' mission of Luke 4.18 'To set at liberty those who are oppressed'? Some churches in Britain across the denominations are responding to the call for social action through their preaching and praxis and are to be commended, but these enterprises tend to be localized, benefiting both minority and majority communities. The present African Caribbean clergy, such as Bishop Jonathan Jackson from the Rock New Testament Church of God, are much more responsive to societal ills within their community than their forebears. They are 'woke' or informed regarding some of the broader historical, socio-economic and political challenges facing Africa and its diaspora. Critics claim that African Caribbean preachers are not acting as the prophetic voice for the black community despite the congregants in these churches being members of the community that it is claimed they are not serving. Unquestionably, more can be done in this arena and preaching plays a critical function in confronting injustice and oppression.

Pentecostal preaching and liberation theology need not be incompatible, and Bridges Johns (2010) advocates a new Pentecostal pedagogy among the oppressed, based on Scripture and the work of the Holy Spirit. Applying the ideas of Brazilian educator Paulo Freire and his theory of *conscientizacao*, Johns see the process of raising the conscience as a prophetic role inspired by the Spirit's work in salvation, sanctification and Spirit baptism that enables Christians to observe the wonders of God in a confusing world. From her perspective, the

Pentecostal approach must follow closely the interrelationship between theory and praxis. Thereby, preaching is in a fluid critical stage, reflecting the revealed Scripture and the existential praxis of the community led by the Holy Spirit. Through the acts of preaching, African Caribbean Pentecostalism can be the major space for social change.

African Caribbean Pentecostalism could be seen as being transformative, if viewed from another angle. Writing in general about BMCs, Adedibu (2012, pp. 104–5) comments on the holistic nature of the worship, liturgy, preaching and music within these churches that 'reflects spontaneity and enthusiasm, producing flexible oral liturgies ... The most important element of these liturgies is the active participation of every member in the congregation.' Significantly, Adedibu claims that these features, including preaching, have 'social and revolutionary implications' because they empower marginalized individuals.

The emphases on 'salvation' and 'radical transformation' (Beckford, 2000) are possibly two of the most positive attributes of African Caribbean Pentecostal preaching. It must also be acknowledged that the Windrush generation were drawn from a variety of Christian traditions including historic churches and they brought their religious customs, practice and of course preaching to the shores of the British Isles and successfully established many churches throughout the country. Generally, men and women from the Windrush generation have passed on to future generations the baton of their spirituality garnered from their respective Caribbean islands. The pursuit of personal holiness remains constant and some of the other-worldliness of early Pentecostalism has been reinterpreted to suit the modern world without compromising on the core message of Jesus Christ. These churches themselves, through their preaching, have undergone a process of transformation in the twenty-first century. Some churches have been able to reach out to the communities in their respective localities and are increasingly appealing to a diverse constituency with the gospel message. Two cases in point are: Faith Dimensions Church in Milton Keynes led by Pastor Glen Ferguson and The New Testament Church of God in Leeds led by Pastor Anthony Parry, the latter with a membership comprising over 30 different nationalities. The hermeneutics of African Caribbean homiletics has paved the way for the plethora of African Pentecostal/Charismatic or new churches and indigenous churches such as those referred to as Fresh Expressions. In these respects the spiritual landscape of the United Kingdom has been greatly impacted by African Caribbean Pentecostal preaching.

Reflection and activities

- Focus on the quotation at the beginning of this chapter: 'Christian faith must go on being translated, must continuously enter into the vernacular culture and interact with it, or it withers and fades' (Walls 2002, p. 29). What are the implications of this quotation for preaching on any aspect of the Christian faith in your particular geographical location? For example, the doctrine of salvation.
- What are the contextual factors that you need to consider in preaching to your congregants?
  (i) Think specifically about the demography of your locality as a context.
  (ii) The context may comprise any of the following congregational make-up, for example, aged, young, single, married, etc. It may also refer to a specific cultural demography, for example, Romanian, Ghanaian, etc.
- What is your understanding of 'prophetic voice' in preaching? It would be useful to write a definition based on your readings in this area.
- Based on your definition, would you describe your own preaching as prophetic?
- Do you think it is important for clergy to be the prophetic voice of their community?
- What might be some of the challenges for them speaking 'prophetically' in your particular context?

Appendix A

Sermon Notes: 'Grace the Gift of Salvation and Your Identity' by Pastor Esther Bonsu for Restoration Fellowship Ministries on Sunday 4 February, 2018

What is grace?

Charis: favour, kindness, a gift/blessing brought to man by God, freely extended to give himself away to people (he is always leaning towards them)
The car ticket analogy

What is salvation?

Deliverance from death
Romans 6.23: 'For the wages of sin *is* death, but the gift of God *is* eternal life.'

The beginning

Adam and Eve
The great deception
Adam was created in the image of God
Had the DNA and significance of God
Walked with God
Talked with God already knew the thoughts of God towards him and his purpose
Satan states; eat the fruit and you will be as wise as God
You were already as wise as God, because he taught you how to think; there were no other influences but God

Jesus steps in

And you *He made alive,* who were dead in trespasses and sins, in which you once walked according to the course of this world, according to the prince of the power of the air, the spirit who now works in the sons of disobedience, among whom also we all once conducted ourselves in the lusts of our flesh, fulfilling the desires of the flesh and of the mind, and were by nature children of wrath, just as the others.
But God, who is rich in mercy, because of His great love with which He loved us, even when we were dead in trespasses, made us alive together with Christ (by grace you have been saved), and raised *us* up together, and made *us* sit together in the heavenly *places* in Christ Jesus, that in the ages to come He might show the exceeding riches of His grace in *His* kindness toward us in Christ Jesus. For by grace you have been saved through faith, and that not of yourselves; *it is* the gift of God, not of works, lest anyone should boast. For we are His workmanship, created in Christ Jesus for good works, which God prepared beforehand that we should walk in them (Ephesians 2.1–10).

- Satan now tempts Jesus in the desert, if you be the son of God ... again attacks his identity and position and God
- Jesus overcomes Satan because it is written that I am ...
- Jesus extends grace to man: I will die so you can live, I will be punished so you can be free
- I will be the ultimate sacrifice so you won't have to work for redemption
- I will be the lamb
- Olden days people had to sacrifice lambs, etc.
- I will step into the darkness so you can be the light
- John 14.6 no man comes to father unless they are called by the spirit
- John 1.12 we have the right to be called children of God
- Romans 8.29 for he who foreknew, he predestined, to be conformed into the image of Christ. We have the right to be formed like Jesus Christ in every way

- We are called into identity and purpose
- The purpose of that identity is to reveal Jesus through us
- For it is no longer I that live but Christ that lives in me
- He revealed you to the Father
- You stand faultless before his throne because of the blood of Jesus; I will be everlasting lamb
- When people sinned they had to bring a sacrifice to symbolize the death of the sin they committed
- Get past being a sinner saved by grace ... you are an heir and he has swopped places with you
- He pleads your case through his blood
- And he purposes you to plead his case with mankind through his grace and love
- We are seated in heavenly places in Christ Jesus – Ephesians 2.6
- Us exemplifying him on earth is the evidence of His works of transformation
- Be not conformed but be transformed by the renewing of your mind – Romans 12.2
- Let the mind that is in Christ be in you – Philippians 2.5
- Sin is an identity issue, it entered through the world when the serpent in Genesis offered the fruit to Eve ... you can become as wise as God
- They were already as wise as God because he walked with God
- Lucifer had an identity issue, he wanted to become greater than God
- So Christ came to redeem our identity, as royalty, as powerful
- Satan again tries to tempt Christ's identity ... if you be the Son of God.
- Mark 16.17

Appendix B

Sermon Transcript: 'Grace the Gift of Salvation and Your Identity' by Pastor Esther Bonsu Presented at Restoration Fellowship Ministries, Birmingham on Sunday 4 February 2018

Explanatory notes for the text:

1. Italics enclosed with round brackets ( ) indicate action, for example, (*hand clapping*). If any further explanation is required regarding the content of the sermon, it is also enclosed with round brackets. For example (*Pentecostal eschatology relating to the mark of the beast found in Revelation 13.16–18*)
2. ***Bold and italics*** indicate where the preacher's statement includes JC, BBT, other language features and stylistic devices such as image making. For example, ***you've knock him out and he is coming back this afternoon to eat rice, peas and chicken and dessert with you.***
3. Identification of specific language features are in **bold** and enclosed with square brackets [ ]. For example [**performer's cue**]. If further explanation is required relating to the preacher's statement, it is also enclosed with square brackets. For example [**JC word *begrudge* means jealousy**].

EB – Pastor Esther Bonsu
CR – Congregational response

EB The word grace in the Greek is the word *Charis* which means favour for those that are writing this down. It means kindness; it means a gift or a blessing brought to man by God freely, extending, to give himself a way to people and it also means he is always leaning to towards mankind.

So I'll read that one more time: grace means favour, it means kindness, it's a gift or a blessing brought to man by God, it is freely extended to give himself a way to people and is always leaning towards mankind.

OK there is this analogy. I have probably used it here before but just to give you a better analogy between mercy and grace **[Goes on to improvise and presentation of self]**.

So mercy if you're in your car and you're doing a hundred miles per hour on a seventy mile per hour road, does everyone get that? The little circle says seventy miles per hour but you're doing your own thing. The police comes eion eion (*sound of police car*) or ambulance. What is the police sound? **[Performer's cue]**.

CR (*Make the sounds of the police car and laughter*)

EB Yeah you know what I mean and the policeman pulls you over and he says listen you are doing a hundred miles per hour on a seventy mile per hour road but I should really fine you and put some points on your licence but this time I am gonna let you go free. I am not gonna charge you. That is mercy. He shows you mercy. He should have punished you but he chose not to punish you that's not grace OK.

This is grace, you're doing a hundred miles per hour on a seventy mile per hour road. Again the police pulls you over and stops you. He says excuse me you're doing a hundred mile per hour on a seventy mile per hour road and I should fine you but I'm not going to fine you I'm going to abolish your ticket and on top of that I'm going give you a hundred pounds so he has not only shown you mercy by abolishing the punishment you did deserve but now he's given you a gift on top of what you didn't deserve so where you deserved punishment he's given you a gift of grace.

CR Jesus, Jesus, Yes, Yes (*hand clapping*)

EB can you imagine doing a hundred miles per hour and the police says here's a pound for every mile you went over, like it's just mind boggling and that's what Jesus came to do. He said that you deserve death but not only am I not going to give you death. I am actually going to give you a seat on my table and give you everlasting life forever to live. Are we getting that?

CR Yeah, yes, yeah.

EB Amen OK. So that is what grace is, that's the difference between when you receive mercy and when you receive grace. So what is salvation, salvation means deliverance, what were we being delivered from? We were being delivered from death. The book of Romans six verse twenty-three says, 'For the wages of sin *is* death but the gift of God *is* eternal life', so Jesus not only pulls you over and says look you're doing a hundred miles per hour, I'm not gonna give you a ticket but ***I'm gonna give you a gift that you will live forever and ever and ever and you will never die and you will reign with me forever*** [**tonal semantics**]. Yeah.

CR Yes.

EB It gets even deeper guys, don't worry that's me just adding a bit of seasoning, you know we gonna now put the chicken in yeah OK, so we have to go back to the book of Genesis. In the beginning right OK so this is the bit I want you to really get so listen intent, ***you know if that possible husband text you, leave the phone on the side, if that beautiful woman text you leave the phone on the side*** [**improvisation**]. You need to listen to this because I feel that the kingdom of God needs to advance in 2018 but we cannot advance a kingdom we don't understand and you need to understand your potential and your right in the kingdom of God to advance it. I am tired of hearing Christians quote beautiful Scriptures, have beautiful feelings in a service but their Monday to Saturday you're depressed. That is not the life you are called to.

CR Ahoh [**paralinguistic feature**] (*hand clapping*).

EB You might as well go back to the world if that is your salvation because you were bought at a price in order to live a life of joy and bear fruit and unless the Bible is a lie then I don't know why we are not living on this level that we should be living in so there is obviously something wrong with us because there is nothing wrong with him.

CR (*Hand clapping*) Yes, Yes.

EB So this is why I need you to listen to me yea. Because the devil is having too much fun in your playground, and he is not paying rent to live in your yard so you need to kick him out today but you can only kick him out when you understand the rights of eviction, if you don't understand the rights of eviction ***you've knock him out and he is coming back this afternoon to eat rice, peas and chicken and dessert with you*** **[BBT and image making]**.

Let's go back to the beginning. In the beginning God created man, man Adam. Adam walked with God yeah, there was no Eve. Adam and God had a relationship. Now psychology say that the first eight years of a child's life are the most important years of their life because it helps to shape their thinking. So I don't know if Adam was born at zero, as a baby but let's just say he was born as a big man yeah. The first thinking patterns that Adam would ever have would have been only from God because there was no other influences in the earth but God's influence, Amen.

CR Amen, amen.

EB So the only mindset he would have had would have been the mindset of God because the only thing he was in relationship with was with God because he actually ran the earth and he was the boss of this earth and he reported back to his boss who was God his father, Amen.

CR Amen.

EB Then Eve comes in to the picture and she is sent to be a helpmate for Adam. He's been given his assignment, when he was created, God gave him a purpose. God now walks in relationship with him for him to fulfil his purpose and he now adds Eve to say continue in the purpose and I will send you help. That was her role but one day Eve was in the garden and now this serpent comes and says hey if you eat this fruit you will become as wise as God. She's now tempted by the fruit. Pause. What did I just say to you? Adam's wisdom was only what God taught him so the only wisdom he ever had in terms of his thinking came from God so the devil came to tempt Eve with something she already had.

CR Come on, come on, come on …

EB I'll say that again so it drops. They already had the wisdom of God because God created their minds and God created their thoughts and he (Adam) knew the thoughts of God concerning them because he was the only voice in their ears. Now comes an annoying voice to say what you think you have, you don't really have. If you eat this fruit you will become as wise as God so now Eve tempts Adam. You should know your enemy's devices. It does not say you should go into a long two-hour conversation with your adversary. If he is under your feet why do you talk to something that is underneath your feet.

CR Thank you Lord.

EB Our Christianity is fickle and you know that the end-times is coming. The systems of this world are trying to squeeze Christians but if you are really plugged into the kingdom of God it is time to ce-le-brate because the darker it gets, ***the brighter light can shine*** **[JC accent]**.

CR (*Hand clapping*) Yes, yes.

EB But you know … oyster card, oyster card is the mark of the beast. Is God too stupid that he cannot tell his own people, he cannot reveal it through his prophets that look don't take this mark but you're sitting here worried about the mark when he said 'I will lead you into all truth.' (*Pentecostal eschatology relating to the mark of the beast found in Revelation 13.16–18*).

CR Yes that's right ...

EB If I am the driver, relax in the passenger side, enjoy the view, enjoy the journey. Take my peace because my peace surpasses your need to understand. There are some things in the earthly realm you will never understand but know in the spiritual realm we are *winning* (stress on *winning*).

CR Yes. Come on.

EB Know who you are. I was telling Pastor X, I got a new job recently and my CEO every minute because I am new, you know I am trying to be in the background, 'Esther do you think I should hire that person?'**[dramatic presentation of self by enacting the voice of CEO]**

How does this woman want me to behave in this office, asking me loud ... 'Esther what do you think of her?' And I'm like yeah, God, can you not just send me an email or maybe we talk afterwards you know. I can see everyone looking **hmhm [paralinguistic feature]**. She got here five minutes and I said to Pastor X maybe I need to distance myself a bit more and he was like hmhm **[paralinguistic feature]**. Don't ever make excuses for who you are. If they're jealous that is their identity issue and not yours. So if she asks you to eat lunch with her, eat lunch in the middle of the office and let other people ***begrudge*** **[JC word *begrudge* means jealousy]**. Because he will prepare a table for you in the presence of your en-emies.
(*Keyboard softly playing in the background*)

We quote it and when he prepares the table everyone is like ***na*** (**no**) **[BBT]**, I do not want to go forward. Pastor wants us to volunteer you know to do ministry but I don't want to be seen **hnhnhnhn [paralinguistic feature]**. Jesus came to be seen. He didn't do the humble servant. Come look pan me [JC]. Look at me. I will do my miracles in the middle of the city and ***mash up your runnings*** **[*mash up* and *runnings* are BBT words meaning to destroy your endeavours]**. Because when you see me, you have seen the father, when you look pan me, you see the father. He is getting glorified as I am being exalted by man. What do you mean you're here to hide? Some of you haven't gone for opportunities because of fear. ***'Oh and Gad, no opportunities coming for me.' What do you mean? Stop moaning. God's like my G, my darling, my babes*** **[JC and BBT]**. I opened ten doors and you decided to choose false humility and not go for the ten doors in the name of Jesus but humility is not thinking less of yourself, it is thinking less of yourself to put other people before yourself.

CR That's right; that's right.

EB But it doesn't mean that you don't take opportunities because as you're take opportunities, your taking opportunities, you're setting other people free who are in the journey that you have overcome to let them know that you can actually attain this place.

CR Come on, that's true.

EB (*Puts on a small voice*) 'Ah you know I need a clear sign.' The sign is on the cross yeah. I need a sign that this is the right ministry. The sign is on the cross. It is finished so now that it is finished, what is your purpose? What are you going to do now? What's your prayer life now? Is it still about your debt because the Bible says if any man lacks wisdom let him ask and he will get it freely. I said 2018 God give me wisdom with my finance, with my relationships, with my job, with my ministry, with my ideas; in every single sphere of my brains, he gives me wisdom, the wisdom of heaven.

CR (*Hand clapping*) and (*keyboard playing softly in the background*)

EB That's my message. I don't know where to take it from here. I came to wake you up. We are in a fixed fight where you have already won so what are you going to do with the victory. But some of you are coming from such a hard background that you have filled your whole life that Christ is saying this is not a battle you can win I've already won it. You're like let me go and fight again and you're fighting thin air because it has already been won. All you need to do is walk in the promises of God and the promises of God will unlock doors that no man can open and no man can shut but it be for God because we say promotion doesn't come from the north, the south, the east or the west. Promotion comes from God. So what are you doing? Honestly what are we doing? This is the bit Auntie Esther comes out. I come to exalt you to your seat. I've come to rattle you that your time is ticking on. How long you've got on this earth?

CR Thank you.

EB The time, the clock is going down. I just buried my cousin thirty-one, she's gone. She didn't have forty to pick a dream, forty-five ... she's gone and I pray that whatever she was put on this earth to do she fulfilled it. Now I don't want you to go home anxious OK God what shall I do? What shall I do? It's not an anxious ting (thing) it is a relationship **ting [BBT]** yeah, yeah.

CR Yes.

EB If I bring it down to like a woman meeting a man. You don't go on the date and be like shall I breathe, shall I not, shall I eat like, shall I this, no you just go in and be yourself.

CR That's right.

EB You chill, you show, ***you flex*** [**BBT** ***flex*** **means relax**]. If he likes it, come tune, come talk to my pastor may be he might put a ring on you know. If not park yourself somewhere else, there's a king on his way and you're holding up the chair yeah. There's a chair over there for Sis Penelope but this chair is for the king, and that's for brothers too.

CR That's right, my Lord.

EB So if you can do that with your earthly wisdom how come you can't run life like that and you've got the truth living on the inside of you. You've got the seed to reproduce yourself living on the inside of you. 'Pastor Carol I just feel so sad Pastor Carol pray for me again Pastor Carol. You pray for me nine months now for depression to leave and it's still there Pastor Carol. Maybe your prayers not strong enough, maybe you're not really my pastor or leader, maybe I need to go and fine (find) another leader who can set me free because the anointing in this church not strong enough because the calling God has on my life Pastor Carol can't handle it' **[Dramatic presentation of self]**, ***because mi not seen freedom since I gat here, oh God*** **[JC accent]**.

CR Glory, glory to God (*hand clapping*).

EB Pastor Carol is not your freedom. You're freedom is in Christ. She is your teacher.

CR (*Hand clapping*). Come on, oh yes.

EB So when she preaches from the front, you take the lesson and you go in the word of God and you make it work for yourself.

CR Yeah, yes, yes.

EB She is not here to work for you. She's here to work for him. You put false responsibility on a human.

CR Jesus.

EB You put false responsibility onto see your future. She told you God said and you keep coming back 'are you sure'. She not a palm reader, she a prophet. She speak once. You lucky she speak twice. No but it's her job to go before God and find out what's going on. No, no, no, no, no *(stated emphatically)*. It's her job to speak what God tells her to speak. It's your job to go on your knees and have a relationship with God about whether you're going left or right. We put too much on our leaders and when they let us down we get ***vex*** with our leader but if you walked in their shoes for ten minutes you wouldn't be able to run the church. **[JC word *vex* means angry/upset]**

CR No way.

EB Because you can't even run your house.

CR Mmmmm fire, ooh, speak the truth, hmmm.

EB Can't run yu yard **[JC word *yard* means house]**. Throw your shoes if you don't want me to talk too much (*aimed at Pastor Carol*).

Pastor Carol's response No, no please go on.

EB I don't want no one sitting there ah cos you're her friend, yeah let me tell you something yeah this is my babe I will fight for her, don't get it twisted. I will fight for her but at the same time I didn't get saved just to become a fool. These two women love you a lot (*referring to Pastor Carol and Prophetess Tamika*).

CR Yeah, that's right. Come on.

EB Every time we go to meetings and dinner they always talk about you lot. Pastor X, ***a lie***? **[JC *a lie* is a rhetorical phrase meaning am I not telling the truth?]**

Pastor X response True, true word.

Like parents, like look at the trophy Tracy got in the race last night and look what Errol got in the spelling bee last month and we're like aah wow teach us more. You know what I mean? **[cockney/BBT]**.

EB That's how they talk about you and your letting the devil come in your head and ***cussing*** them when you were never born to fight flesh and blood. Submit to leadership **[JC/BBT phrase *cussing* means reprimanding]**.

CR Amen, yes.

EB That word (submission) is horrible. If you're like me I wanna do my own ting. I run my own life. ***I'm a big woman*** **[JC phrase meaning mature adult]**, but if Jesus or God didn't see it fit to put leaders above us for us to submit to then he wouldn't have written it. Why waste your time putting a system that doesn't work. The system works. Church hurt is real. I come from it, Pastor Carol, Prophetess Tamika know my story but just because one church hurt me don't mean that every church gonna ***mash me up*** **[JC phrase *mash me up* means devastation]**.

CR (*Hand clapping*) That's right, that's right.

EB And even that church didn't mash me up because the blood has been spilt. My redemption is in his hands not in no man's hands.

CR That's right, Amen.

EB So submit. I struggled with submission. I struggled with it because I want to do me, but when I was doing me I was mashing up my life so God saw it fit to put shepherds in front of me so they can see the wolf coming from afar and save my life. Put their lives in front to fight off the wolf to save me; we're sheep. All we're here to do is yam **[BBT word meaning to eat]**.

CR Glory, glory, glory.

EB They teach, we yam (eat) what they give us and we're full. **You no [BBT phrase].** We're blessed to have leaders that care. I'm telling you, you lot ain't been to certain *churches*. You lot are blessed to have these two leaders so if you need to apologize to them, apologize because sometimes breakthrough can come through 'I am sorry.' It does not always have to be halamashanda (imitating speaking in tongues). It can be a character thing. That's all I came here to say.

CR Thank you, praise the Lord, Amen.

Appendix C

Sermon Transcript: 'Elevated by the Power of God' by Pastor Nathan Turner Presented at The Rock New Testament Church of God, Birmingham 20 January, 2018

Explanatory notes for the sermonic text:

1. Italics enclosed with round brackets ( ) indicate action, for example, (*hand clapping*). If any further explanation is required regarding the content of the sermon, it is also enclosed with round brackets. For example (*The term cross over appears to be from Africa, meaning to enter into a new year*).
2. ***Bold and italics*** indicate where the preacher's statement includes JC, BBT, other language features and stylistic devices such as image making. For example, ***eight a dem have the bag ready, stand at the door***.
3. Identification of specific language features are in **bold** and enclosed with square brackets [ ]. For example, **[performer's cue]**. If further explanation is required relating to the preacher's statement, it is also enclosed with square brackets. For example, **[JC phrase *life case* meaning with everything inside of me]**.

NT – Pastor Nathan Turner
CR – Congregational response

NT You look fantabulous today. My wife is going to read the Bible. (*His wife reads 1 Corinthians 6.16–20*). And verse 14 says God raised the Lord and will also raise us up by his power. Just turn to your neighbour and give them the topic for this discussion, which is: ***Elevated by the power of God*** **[performer's cue].**

CR Elevated by the power of God.

NT You're not putting on your preacher's voice on today, so turn to your other neighbour and say, 'elevated by the power of God' **[performer's cue]**.

CR Elevated by the power of God.

NT Amen. We are two weeks into 2018 and we're thankful that we have been able to cross over from last year into this. (*The term cross over appears to be from Africa, meaning to enter into a new year*). Many people have a tradition that when they cross over into the new year they make a new year's resolution and now by this time, two weeks in, they are reviewing their decision, whether it be to lose weight, to cut out sweets and chocolate, to exercise more, I don't know what the new year's resolution is, to quit smoking whatever, but by this time they are reviewing whether they made the resolution in a moment of madness because it seems like they have reneged or gone back on their new year's resolution. January is a month in which we see increases in gym membership, all paid up. Everybody says for sure I'm going to the gym and by the end of January gym membership is being paid and nobody is not ***seeing you at the*** **gym [stated in JC accent]**. I used to work at Sure Start children's centres; within the month we saw that this was the most busiest time for domestic violence as people had crossed over into the new year and say 'this is going to be a new day for the family, we're going to do this, we're going to do that' and couple weeks in all of the promises have gone back and we are back to business as usual. Just turn to your neighbour very quickly and tell them if your new year's resolution is still going **[performer's cue]**.

CR (*Individual audience members talk to each other*)

NT Are you still working on it? They say confession is good for the soul. Some of you need to fine (find) an altar because you have not been to the gym at ***atall*** **[JC]**. (*Chuckles to himself*). Paul in the Scripture that we read is writing to the Corinthian church and he's addressing several issues and if you read through Corinthians you see he jumps from one subject to the other. He'll talk about, as he does in this chapter, people suing each other, taking each other to court when they are members of the church. When they have an issue they fall out, they bump cars and instead of sorting it out among themselves, they have gone into the court of the land and suing each other. He says that this is not a practice that you should be doing as Christians. You must work together and sort out your disagreements and he goes on throughout the chapter and now he addresses the issue of ... morality and he's asking in the first part of the chapter for you to raise or to elevate or to uplift the way you enjoy your relationships with your bother and sister in the church, raise your game (*At this point NT raises his chest* – **[dramatic presentation of self]**.

Do not do the things that the world do because when they have a disagreement they go straight to the court but Paul is saying elevate the way that you conduct your relationships and do it differently. In the second half of the chapter he says now I want you to elevate your morality, the way that you practice your Christianity, the way that you practice your life, the decisions that you make, it must be elevated, it must be raised. It must look totally different from the man who walks down the road and does not profess Christ. There must be a difference between you and them in the way that you live your moral life. Among the Christians there was a practice before the outbreak of the gospel of having sexual sin. They would use prostitutes in the temple and it would be an OK thing around the Corinthian city to engage in sexual immorality with prostitutes. So Paul is saying now that you have found Christ and you have come into the kingdom of God and you know who he is that is the risen Christ and Saviour you cannot practice sexual immorality again. Flee from these things. The Scripture says 'flee from youthful lust that corrupts the body and the mind'. The

Scripture says that when you do such a practice you don't just only sin against another person, against God but you also sin against your body and he goes on to say, 'know ye not that your body is the temple of the Lord'. You house the Holy Spirit within you so you must protect yourself in your spiritual life and in your moral life in order to protect yourself physically, because people have this idea if they do whatever they wanna do and exercise themselves that they are not really damaging their physical body, but the Bible says that 'the wages of sin is death' and so if you practice a life of sin you are killing yourself not just spiritually, but you are physically killing yourself. Am I preaching good things? The Bible says that Paul talks to the Corinthian church. He is writing a letter; he is not with them as the founder of the church he is on another missionary journey, but he is writing back to them teaching them how to behave themselves and the opening clause in verse twelve it says that, or thirteen that I will not be controlled by anything no passion, no desire, no person, no external thing, no internal thing is going to control me and so he makes, like you and I, he makes a resolution, he makes a determination in his mind's eye that I will not be controlled by anything. Paul had the power of a strong will. Turn to your neighbour and say: 'Paul had the power of a strong will' [**performer's cue**].

Like we've just discussed we make new year's resolutions and not just at new year but at various times in our lives we will make a resolution. We will make a determination in our minds to say that we are going to achieve this. We set a goal, we set a vision we put things in place, we pay for things, we call up friends, ***we do whatever we gotta to do*** [**BBT**] because we have made up in our minds that we are gonna do something so we have willed it, we have made a resolution so willpower is important in elevating your life. There are three things that we are gonna talk about from the Scripture. First is the power of will. Many times we put this down and we denigrate it to something that should not be engaged in, but you have to develop a mindset and an understanding, a cognitive understanding that you are going to develop yourself and you're going to push yourself forward. You have to make a determination in your mind, first because you cannot engage in any kind of practice unless you have made up in your mind to do it. We sang the song 'I will exalt you', believe you me some of us came in here with no intention to exalt the Lord. We come because it's Sunday and on Sunday this is what we do. We come to church because my mum or my dad grew me up in that fashion and so in the morning you get yourself dressed. You ***spruce up yourself*** and you come to the house of the Lord because your motivation is routine [***spruce up yourself is a JC phrase*** **which does not appear to be used frequently in modern English and means to make one's appearance look attractive by the clothes worn**].

But I don't know about you or your perception of what is the reason you should come into church for, but you see when I woke up this morning I knew that I didn't wake up myself. I knew that the breath that I breathed is borrowed. I live on borrowed time. I only have a certain amount of time to exist on this earth and believe you me any moment that I have, any moment that is afforded me to come before the great presence of the Lord, I will exalt him. ***Aaaa*** **[paralinguistic feature].** You not preaching with me today? *(Request for responses)*

CR (*Hand clapping*)

NT There is a determination in my mind and in my heart that my life, not just when I come here on a Sunday but the entirety of my life must exalt the name of the Lord Jesus Christ. (*At this point the delivery becomes louder*). I live in an atmosphere of worship. When me and my wife are at home with the children sometimes Fred Hammond (an American gospel artist) has to come on and there has to be a worship session going on. When I'm among my friends, among my colleagues the way that I live, the way that I talk in conversation must be a worship unto the Lord (*NT bends down*) **[presentation of self]**. Because I have made a decision in my life. I think it was October of 1996 when I made a decision that I am going to serve the Lord. Not just for that moment because there was an emotional reaction to what the preacher was saying, but I knew that God had called my life. I had a call upon my life. I knew that I was a sinner and I need to make a change and so I will exalt the name of the Lord. When you have engaged your will you have then made a focus and the problem is, Brother Gerald, is that when you make a resolution to go to the gym you get distracted. You drive to the gym but you see the KFC logo [**humour**].

CR (*Audience laughs*).

NT You see the golden arches of McDonalds and the ***light start to shine in you eye*** [**JC**] ***and you sey hol on mek me jus mek a lickle turn*** (*hold on let me just make a little turn*) [**JC**]. ***Let me just pas dere before me go to di gym*** [**code-switching from SE to JC**].

When you engage your will you have a focus and you cannot be distracted. And believe you and me anytime you make a decision just know that the enemy is going to come with every living distraction to push your mind away from the decision you have made, but the Bible tells me it is with the mind that we serve the Lord and so the mind has to be engaged and maintained in your service, in your worship, in whatever you are doing, you have to keep your decision. You have to engage your will. ***Sometimes the problem that we have in church you know*** [**JC accent**] is that people come into the arena of church and ***we check our brain at the door*** [**Birmingham accent**]. We come and we have a numb experience in the house of the Lord, numb experience in engaging with people in our relationships and sometimes we dumb ourselves down because we do not have the ability and that is what it is about engaging your will. It's the mental capacity, it's the mental focus, the mental wherewithal to know that you have decided to do something but you have to be able to back, back all of the things that come as a distraction to your mind. So the Bible says that the enemy 'comes in as a thief in the night' and in the garden of the church where there are good fruits growing he plants tares among us and sometimes it's because we are unaware of what's going on. We have lost our focus and we have disengaged our will but let me tell you something

if we are going to elevate the fellowship,
if you are going to elevate ministry,
if we are going to elevate our worship,
if we are going to elevate your life your will must continually be engaged **[repetition: lists].**

Just turn to you neighbour and say, 'Lord touch my mind' **[performer's cue].**

CR Lord touch my mind.

NT Turn to the other neighbour and say, 'Lord touch my mind.'

CR Lord touch my mind.

NT It is with the mind, the Scripture says that we serve the Lord. The Scripture says, Paul says like Jesus that we are going to be raised like Jesus, raised with power and willpower in itself is a good thing. It gives us focus as we have already discussed and there are instances where *I heard a story where a mother engaged in a car crash and she was flung from the car but her child was still in the car and by sheer willpower alone, beloved baby is in the car she turned the car in order to get her baby out* **[improvisation].**

So such is the power of will when you fully engage it. But you know something, willpower is great but it is limited when it exists on its own. You made up your mind and it's great for you to do that in order for you to have focus but you must also have the power of desire. Willpower on its own is great but is better if you have the power of desire or the power of passion. Oftentimes you can see people who have functioning alone and you know them because they are your partners at work. You have the job share or in your team. You're all doing the work and you know that person their heart is not in it. Because the job is not done to fulfilment you have to go around them and pick up the pieces what they left. They clock out if they are suppose to finish at five, at four forty *eight a dem have the bag ready, stand at the door* [JC] waiting for the minutes to go down, their heart is not in it. They have no passion, they have no desire, they have no unction to do the job and so they are just clocking up the wages. And if you are in an industry like mine, education or in health or in social work or anything like that, you can't just do the job because sometimes lives are at stake. You have to have some passion in the midst of what you are doing. ***Hrhr*** **[paralinguistic feature]** Am I talking to somebody today?

CR Yes, hmhm.

NT Yes they made up their mind to do the job. They, they fill out the application like everybody else and went through the job interview and the performance management. They say the right thing and do just enough to cover their own back but you see the person that have a desire and a passion to do that job whether it be five thirty, whether it be six o'clock they're gonna stay until the job is finished. They go to the nth degree, they sacrifice themselves. They sometimes sacrifice things because they know they have a calling on their life to function in this arena. (*Stated loudly*) And so whatever it cost they are going to get the job done. That's the power of desire.

Oh Jesus sometimes we want to change and I'm looking at my life as I examine the theme of elevate. What do I want to achieve? How do I want to elevate my life, elevate my family, elevate myself at work and in my ministry. How am I going to do this in 2018? But if I do not engage my passion in these things I'm gonna do a half-hearted job. And the Bible says to me if you are neither hot or neither cold that God will spew you out. Lukewarmness is not going to get anywhere, mediocrity is a sin before God, when excellence is possible; that's why my former bishop, Dr Ryan, would say mediocrity is sin where excellence is possible. If you can excel in that arena then do it under the anointing of God, because God has given you the power to do so. And so if you are to elevate your life, elevate your family in 2018, then we've got to engage in the power of passion, the power of desire. And sometime we don't fulfil our goals and dreams because we are full of fear. We have put it out there, we have made a statement into the atmosphere

I am going to go to university, I am going to sign up for this job, I am going to, gonna do whatever it is. I'm gonna run the marathon in 2018. We've put our name tag onto this achievement, but when it comes down to the brass tacks of what it takes to run a marathon, we think Lord have mercy. We start to backtrack because we are not able to go through the pain and burden of what passion brings. I was reading the scripture Adrian (*referring to someone in the congregation*) and I was wondering. Paul is talking to the Corinthian church. They fell into immoral behaviour. They are using prostitutes and engaging in sex in which they shouldn't do as Christians and in the middle of this clause he says, he talks about the resurrection of Jesus Christ. He's telling the people to behave themselves but in the middle of it he says that Jesus was raised and he will also raise us with power so I'm saying to myself why would Paul talk about the resurrection when people need to behave themselves in their immorality. Paul uses the resurrection as an example of what it was to have the passion and the burden upon your life. For the Bible says that Jesus Christ was crucified on a cross and on that cross. He had to before he reached Golgotha, he has to carry the cross towards Calvary's hill. You've watched the film they call it *The Passion of the Christ* when he was scourged. He was whipped, he had the crown of thorns placed upon his head, but he had to carry that crown on his head as a burden. And the Bible says, I think it is in Hebrews. It says a very interesting thing. It says 'he despised the shame'. ***hmhm*** **[paralinguistic feature]**.

(*Stated very loud*) Oh Jesus he despised the shame but he endured it for the joy that was set before him, oh God. Jesus knew that if he didn't go through the cross then lives would be lost in eternity. We would have no means of salvation, man could not be brought back unless he go through the crucifixion and so even though he had the scourge, even though he was whipped they said some thirty-nine times, they said even though he had to wear a crown of thorns, even though they plucked out of his beard, even though they stripped him naked. The Bible says he endured the pain of having a passion. The power of his passion drove him to the cross.

(*Stated loudly*) So Paul uses the resurrection and in this clause to say that power is in this passion. He is saying you are taking your feelings of sexual arousal and you're going and making that feeling push you into madness. Some of you are eating too much. Paul says because you are letting the hunger, the desire, the passion for food overwhelm you.

(*Stated very loudly*) But Paul says use the power of passion in the right way. Don't be controlled by your lust. Don't be controlled by your greed, but rather let the power of passion raise you up in your mortal bodies, raise you up in your spirit, raise you up in your mind's eye that you can fulfil the will of God. (*At this point NT is jumping up and down and continues in a very loud voice*). Am I talking sense to anyone in here? Paul says look at it, look at the physical manifestation what passion is. Sometimes we use this Caribbean phrase ***you dead fi hungry*** [**JC: innocent turn of phrase meaning you are starving to death**]. You have not eaten one thing from *marning* (morning). By one, two o'clock ***yu sey to yu colleague 'I am dead fi hungryyy'*** [JC]. Oh, woi Jesus I wonder if you understand what I am saying in here today? The physical drive Peter? (*Referring to someone in the congregation*). To open up the fridge and go ***tek out las night dinner*** [JC], warm it up in the microwave. You just can't wait to get home to tastes Sis Lorna food (*presumably Peter's wife*). That physical drive Paul says that you teking and engaging in sex, don't use it in that way but know that the same drive that you have can be the same drive to love God and to serve him (*shouts on the last clause*).

Sis Annette please pass on to bishop (*referring to Bishop Jonathan Jackson, the bishop of the church*), don't let, don't place anyone in my team that don't have no passion. Please tell him Sis Annette because I can't deal with it. Am a patient man. I'm a loving man but you see one thing I can't stand, if you're gonna do something, do it with the best of your ability. You see the reason why I jump in church Sister Yvonne, you know sometime you have to tie me down to my seat, you know but I have passion for Jesus Christ, but you know when I was growing up I had passion for football ... Chris (*referring to someone in the congregation*). When Liverpool and John

Barnes bend one in from the corner ***yu wan si me*** (you want to see me) [JC]. (*At this point NT jumps up and down to demonstrate his reaction to the goal scored*). **Yes [shouts very loudly] *You wan si mi run up and down yes*** [JC] (*Jumps up and down and runs at the front of the church to demonstrate his reaction again*) **[dramatic presentation of self]**. Yes Barnsie (*reference to football player John Barnes*). If me a do dat for football (*NT bends his body down and stops in the middle of the sentence signalling on-T, that is call–response feature that something is on point and what more can one say about the matter*). (*Keyboard starts playing softly at this time*).

CR (*Hand clapping*)

NT If I am doing that for football (stress on ball) ... (*Very loud*) What more would I do for Jesus Christ who died to save me from my sin, who redeems me every day. (*Uses one of his feet in a kicking fashion*). Who puts food on my table, clothes on my back. I must lift up his name with power and with passion. (*Jumps up and down while placing his hands on an enclosed raised altar*).

CR (*Individual congregants stand up and clap their hands*)

NT Sometimes I come in here I just don't even want to hear. Just don't want to hear the moderator to start the service. I don't want to hear nothing. I just want to get into prayer and get into worship quick time. Quick time. Sometime the moderator up here ***pumping and pumping*** **[phrase *pumping* in this sense means to encourage congregants to engage in worship if the service is flat or lacks vitality]**. The poor praise and worship team ***afi lif hunno* up** (have to lift everyone up). They have to wipe ***unu*** (everyone) ***down***. They hafi (have to) cajole you. **[JC phrases and use of metaphors for encouraging congregants to engage in worship] *Come-come, come-come, come-come* [*come-come* is reduplication meaning 'come on']**. (*Shouts very loudly indeed*) No! Has not God done ***anything for you*** **[screams]**. I lang (long) for the day that when I come into the house of the Lord I jus walk tru (through) the door and feel the anointing nobody can't run no service, jus glad he's (*NT screams*) lifted up. The cloud of his glory just engulf everybody and they have to lift him (*NT continues to shout and at this point and speaks in tongues*). ***Let the passion arise. Let the passion arise. Let the passion arise*** **[simple repetition]**. (*Keyboard plays softly on each of the following phrases*) The passion for Jesus. The passion for God.

CR (*Loud wailing, individuals stand up*)

NT The passion for his work. The passion for his power. Brother Wallace (*referring to someone in the congregation*), the problem is you see we have people coming in and they want to receive. They want to receive from God but they don't want to give ***noten*** to God you know **[word 'nothing' pronounced as *noten* in BBT]**. (*Chuckles* and *bends down slightly*) **[dramatic presentation of self]** Oh Jesus but my life. All of my training, all of my schooling, all of the way that I was brought up I was taught to serve the Lord. (*Begins rowing action*) **[dramatic presentation of self]** Serve the Lord with gladness. Come before his presence with thanksgiving. Oh my God enter his gates with praise, with thanksgiving in your heart. (*Rowing action becomes more intense*) I will enter into his courts with praise. I will be thankful to him and I will bless (*NT screams*) his holy mighty, matchless, wonderful, exhorted [exalted] name, holy name.
(*Keyboard plays louder and together with drums*)
(*Stated loudly*) Let the people praise him.
(*Stated loudly*) Let the people praise him.
(*Stated very loudly and screams on praise him*) Let the people praise him.
[Simple repetition and crescendo effect]
(*NT Jumps up and down and all around*) **[dramatic presentation of self]**
Ooo ooo, ooo, ooo, ooo **[paralinguistic feature, African retention]**
(*NT Jumps around*), ***ooo, ooo.***
(*NT waves his arms around vigorously*) **[dramatic presentation**

of self]
[Sound and motion between NT and congregants]
(*NT places one arm around his back and waves the other arm around vigorously*)
(*Keyboard and drums playing fairly loudly*)

CR (*Many individuals stand up, and there are shouts of hallelujah*)
(*Keyboard and drums playing softly*)
(*NT walks around the platform for several seconds and wipes his face with purple handkerchief*)

CR (*Individuals walking at the front of the church in the spirit shouting hallelujah*). **[Sound and motion continues]**
***Wooo, wooo, wooo, wooo, wooo, wooo, wooo, wooo* [paralinguistic features]**
(*NT jumps up and down on one spot and at the same time waves arms vigorously*)

NT Chris praise him, Chris praise him, Tina praise him, Danny praise him, Angie praise him, Adrian praise him. (*NT waves his right hand*) Marie praise him. (*Keyboard and drums play louder*) ***Wooi* [paralinguistic feature]**

(*Many congregants are in the Spirit and come to the front of the church with hands lifted up and walking from one end to the other*)

NT Mother, mother, mother (*maybe NT's mother or an elderly woman of the church*). Can I have some more on this mic? (microphone) Can I have some more on this mic up here?
I can't move unless I bless him right here. And some of you are sat on your seat still
I'm preaching out my ***life case*** and you're still not listening to me **[JC phrase *life case* meaning with everything inside me]**.
(*NT screams*) Get up and worship the Lord.
(*Keyboard, drums and guitar playing*)

NT Oh Jesus, ***Oooi, Oooi, Oooi, Oooi, Oooi*** **[paralinguistic features]**. I feel an anointing for breakthrough in this place. Oh God, if only you would stretch your hands, if only you would lift your voices. If only you would extend yourself just a minute, just a minute, just a minute, just a minute, just a minute **[simple repetition]**. I say the walls are gonna come breaking down. Oh every barrier is gonna be removed if you would just worship the Lord. ***Oooi*** **[paralinguistic feature]**. (*NT breathes heavily through microphone*) ***Hey, hey, hey, hey*** **[paralinguistic features]**. Come on, come on, come on. Everybody, everybody, everybody stand. Just hold it for a minute (*reference to musicians to play softly*). Everybody stand if you are physically able to stand then please stand ***wooo, wooo*** (*NT wipes face with handkerchief*) ***wooo, woo*** **[paralinguistic features and presentation of self and crescendo effect]**

CR Jesus, Jesus ...

NT The Bible declares that the disciples were waiting on Jesus and they were all in the upper room and the Bible says this funny thing that they were all in one accord. The reason that we play with Sunday morning and Sunday worship is that we have forgotten the principle of being in one accord. You see corporate worship it means Brother Adrian you are going through some thing you know and by rights the weight that is upon you. It means that you can't worship but you see when you link with me and I feel the fire, I pass the fire on to you my brother and ***it's you this week but it's gonna be me next week*** **[proverbial expression meaning it will be your turn soon]**.

But if we are continually lifting up ourselves then nobody has to be left behind Brother Paul. Oh God. New Testament Church of God, the Rock. Can you lift up the name of Jesus in one accord (*jumps up and down vigorously*). One accord, one accord, one accord, one Lord, one master, one Saviour, one baptism, one Spirit **[crescendo effect]**. (*Keyboard, drums and guitar playing softly*). Elevate the naaammm (name) of the Lord.

CR (*Individual congregants walk around the praise and worship team*)

NT Tek (take) a seat, tek a seat. Have to behave myself, the bishop just come in (*At this point the bishop walks in*) ***wooo, wooo*** **[paralinguistic feature]**. The power of passion, Paul is telling us, it is such a driving force. When you're in the world, there's a Scripture in Luke I think it is that says the children of darkness are more wiser than the children of light. What does that mean Simeon? It means that when you're in the world every kind of darkness and slackness ***yu gan in a it*** (*You have gone into it*) **[JC]**.

And you throw yourself in it. Every weight is gone, every energy is gone, whatever resource you have you throw yourself in it, but it seems like when you come into the light you want to dip yu toe (*NT demonstrates this by tentatively stepping one foot on the ground*). The Spirit of God is moving pastor but everybody want to ***oooo*** **[paralinguistic feature]**. I can't tek it yu know. No it's too much (*NT walks down from the stage and stands in front of the lectern*). I heard one Old Testament prophet sey (say) the water came up to my ankle bones and then the water came up to my knee bones and then it came up to the waist bone and then it came up to the shoulder Sister Price. (*NT walks towards Sister Price, a fairly elderly woman*) I want to be under the flow. (*They both briefly dance gracefully, in unison*) I want to be fully baptized, fully immersed, fully lost in the presence of the Almighty. (*Sister Price spins around once*) (*NT returns to the lectern*)

NT Sometimes we don't engage in our passion because we are full of fear of what the cost is gonna be but as Jesus was raised on the cross and first had to carry that cross so do we. We have to carry the burden of our passion before we can be elevated. When you in a position where you full of fear of what's going on. In first John, I think it is the Scripture says that when you are full of fear you cannot do anything, but when perfect love comes **it *casteth out*** ... (*very short pause*).

CR [**completer statement ...** ***casteth out fear***]

NT I have some people that know their Bible. When perfect love comes Sister Turner it casteth out all fear. So he says for the love of God in that Scripture, it says for the love of God casteth out all fear. Now Paul we can interpret for the love of God in three different ways because there is no word in the Greek for *Aff*. As it appears in the Greek it says Agape Christos the unconditional love but there is no clause in the Greek that says *Aff*. So it could be the love that God has for us casteth out all fear or it could be the love that we have for God casteth out all fear.

(*NT chuckles to himself*). So let's play with this thing Sister Yvonne. If it is the love of God that he has for us that casteth out all fear then we have to understand that the love of God means that there are times of chastisement Brother Peter because the Bible says that God, those who God love he chasenth and the clause in first John says for the love of God restrains us ... sorry, sorry let me get it right. I'm mixing up two Scriptures. The Scripture says that the love of God casteth out all fear, that's a different verse from what I'm saying. In first John it says for the love of God constraineth us so the love that God has for us can constrain us but to make that clause right Simmy, it constrain is an action from the inwards outward. When God chastises us it is outward inward because he puts us in a situation in which we are restraint so if it is therefore the love of God that constraineth us. To be right if it was God's love we would have to say for the love of God restrains us. So then Adrian for the love of God must mean the love of God that I have for God constrains.

CR Praise God, praise God.

NT Paul, when you are constraint. If we look to the original Latin it means there are two things that are intertwined that then pull. Restraint is a pull from the outside but constraint means that you have a pull from the inside and so the love of God constraineth us means that the Spirit of God inside of us works with my willpower and it works with my ***desire power and added to it the Holy Ghost power*** **[word play on power].** When I'm in a situation where they're telling me all kine (kind) of foolishness and drawing me away from God, putting me in the place of temptation, putting me in the place of trials because I have a love for God there is an inner pulling (*NT begins to shout on the last clause*)

CR (*Stand on their feet*) Yeah, come on ...
(*Keyboard plays softly*).

NT My conscience will not let me go away from the will of God. That is why David said 'Thy word have I hid in my heart that I will not sin against you.' If you want to be elevated in 2018 you've got to engage your willpower. ***You've got to engage your passion power, but you've also got to engage the Holy Ghost power*** **[tonal semantics]**. You've got to get the word and let it soak into your life until it becomes an instinct to do the will of God. You don't even have to think about it. (*NT jumps up and down*) You don't have to question it. You don't have to cry out. You don't have to phone a friend. You don't have to take fifty–fifty but the Holy Ghost power that is inside of you works on your willpower. (*NT jumps up and down*) Both to will and to do the power of God. Both to will and to do the purpose of God. Both to will and to do (*NT screams on the last phrase*) **[dramatic and crescendo effect]**.

CR Praise God, Amen.

NT 2018 I am engaging my mind around this topic. I'm going to be elevated. I'm gonna elevate my family. Any time you're around me, I'm gonna speak words that are gonna elevate you. I ain't got time to gossip bout you. I ain't got time to pull you down. ***I ain't got time to chat about ya*** **[stated in Birmingham accent and *ya* is BBT]**, ***rubbish and foolishnes*** **[JC accents]**. I've got to elevate you. I've got to lift you up. This is the calling of God on my life to give you pastoral care, to give you ***brothership*** **[creative use of language]**, to give you friendship,

to give you sonship, to lift you up, lift you up above every shadow. Let every darkness come down.
Let the light of Jesus be risen upon you.
Let the devil be bound in the name of Jesus and let the Holy Spirit have free reign to lift up my son, to lift up my daughter,
To lift up my unsaved step-daughter,
To lift up my grandchildren into salvation,
To lift up my colleagues into the righteous ways.
[repetition: lists]
Hold the hands of your neighbour in this place, Oh God. 'You are my strength, you are my strength' (*stating the line of a gospel song*). Hallelujah. Thank you Jesus. 'You are my strength like no other.'

(*Praise and worship team stand and sings the song softly*: '*You are my strength, strength like no other* … ')

NT I tried willpower by myself. I tried to push it through with passion but I couldn't do it. I needed the Holy Ghost to work on my will, to work on my passion so I could be elevated. Hallelujah, hallelujah. Come on let's lift up the name of Jesus. Hallelujah, hallelujah.

(*The praise and worship team sing louder and NT joins in*)

NT Come on lift those hands and give him praise. Hallelujah, hallelujah. Thank you Jesus.

CR Amen, hallelujah, Jesus, Jesus.

(*NT continues singing with praise and worship team*)

NT 'God lift us up' (*stating a line from the song as the Praise and worship team continue singing*).

End of sermon

(*NT proceeds to make an altar call*) …

Reflection and activities

- Focus on Appendices A and B. The differences between the written format and the actual presentation of Pastor Esther's sermon are striking. Can you outline these differences in terms of the structure and themes covered? In what other ways does the presentation diverge from the written text?
- Pastor Esther uses a number of stylistic devices in the presentation of the sermon (Appendix B). Some have already been referenced in the Appendix. Comment on any others that you can identify.
- Pastor Nathan (Appendix C) utilizes the range of stylistic devices, many of which have been identified. Can you identify any other features? What are your views on the effectiveness of these stylistic components for presenting the overall theme of his sermon?
- How far do you think Pastor Nathan's sermon deviates from Buttrick's episodic preaching?
- Can you choose three occasions when Pastor Nathan appears to improvise in the text?
- Compare and contrast the sermons of Pastors Nathan and Esther in appendices B and C. Comment on the general themes of each sermon. Are there any significant stylistic differences between? How does each preacher use language to convey theological themes? What do the themes covered suggest about their theology? Comment on any other differences you observe.

Bibliography

Abrahams, R. D. (1972) The Literary Study of the Riddle. *Texas Studies in Literature and Language* (14), pp. 177–97.

Ackah, W., Dodson, J. E. and Smith, D. R. (eds) (2017) *Religion, Culture and Spirituality in Africa and the African Diaspora*. New York/ Abingdon, Oxon: Routledge, pp. 115–28.

Adedibu, A. Babatunde (2012) *Coat of Many Colours: The Origin, Growth, Distinctiveness and Contributions of Black Majority Churches to British Christianity*. London: Wisdom Summit.

Aldred, J. (2000) *Sisters with Power*. London: Continuum.

Aldred, J. (2005) *Respect: Understanding Caribbean British Christianity*. Peterborough: Epworth.

Aldred, J. and Ogbo, K. (eds) (2010) *The Black Church in the 21st Century*. London: Darton, Longman and Todd.

Aldred, J. (2010) The Holy Spirit and the Black Church. In Aldred, J. and Ogbo, K. (eds) *The Black Church in the 21st Century*. London: Darton, Longman and Todd.

Alexander, E. (2011) *Black Fire: One Hundred years of African American Pentecostalism*. Downers Grove, Illinois: InterVarsity Press.

Alexander, V. (1996) *'Breaking Every Fetter?' To What Extent has the Black Led Church in Britain Developed a Theology of Liberation*. PhD Dissertation. Warwick: University of Warwick.

Alim, S. and Smitherman, G. (2012) *Articulate while Black: Barack Obama, Language and Race in the US*. Oxford: Oxford University Press.

Alleyne, M. (1980) *Comparative Afro-American: An Historical-Comparative Study of English-based American Dialects of the New World*. Ann Arbor, MI: Karoma Publishers.

Alleyne, M. (1989) *The Roots of Jamaican Culture*. London: Pluto Press.

Alleyne, M., Faraclas, N., Walick, D., Ortix, L. and Geigel, W. (2004) *The Missing Spanish Creoles and the Role of Political Economy in Creole Genesis*. Paper presented at the 15th Biennial Conference of the Society for Caribbean Linguistics, Curacao.

Anderson, A. (2013) *To the Ends of the Earth: Pentecostalism and the Transformation of World Christianity*. Oxford: Oxford University Press.

Anderson, A. (2014) *An Introduction to Pentecostalism* (second edition). New York: Cambridge University Press.

Archer, L. (2009) *The 'Black' Middle Classes and Education: Parents and Young People's Construction of Identity, Values and Educational Practices*. Paper presented to British Educational Research Association (BERA). University of Manchester.

Archer, L. (2011) Constructing Minority Middle-Class Identity: An Exploratory Study with Parents, Pupils and Young Professionals. *Sociology* 45 (1), pp. 134–51.

Asamoah-Gyadu, J. K. (2004) *African Charismatics: Current Developments Within Indigenous Pentecostalism in Ghana*. Studies of Religion in Africa: 27. Leiden: Brill.

Bailey, B. L. (1966) *Jamaican Creole Syntax*. Cambridge: Cambridge University Press.

Bauer, E. and Thompson, P. (2006) *Jamaican Across the Atlantic*. Kingston: Ian Randle Publishers.

Beckford, R. (2000) *Dread and Pentecostal*. London: SPCK.

Beckford, R. (2013) *Documentary as Exorcism: Resisting the Bewitchment of Colonial Christianity*. London and New York: Continuum.

Bernard-Allan, V. Y. (2016) *It is not Good to be Alone: Singleness and the Black Seventh-Day Adventist Woman*. PhD Dissertation. London: The UCL Institute of Education.

Bernstein, B. (1971) *Class, Codes and Control*. New York: Schocken Books.

Bickerton, D. (1981) *Roots of Language*. Ann Arbor, MI: Karoma Publishers.

Blauner, Robert (1970) Black Culture: Myth or Reality? In Whitten, N. E. and Szwed, J. F. (eds) *Afro-American Anthropology: Contemporary Perspectives*. New York: Free Press, pp. 347–66.

Bledsoe, Judith (2006) *Stitching Orality into the Textual Quilt in Derek Walcott's Omeros* (2006) Theses, Dissertations, Professional Papers. Paper 3673.

Bowler, K. (2013) *Blessed: A History of the American Prosperity Gospel*. Oxford: Oxford University Press.

Brathwaite, E. (1984) *History of the Voice*. London: New Beacon Books.

Bridges Johns, C. (2010) *Pentecostal Formation: A Pedagogy among the Oppressed*. Eugene, Oregon: Wipf and Stock Publishers.

Brodgon, L. (2015) *The New Pentecostal Message: An Introduction to the Prosperity Movement*. Eugene, Oregon: Cascade Books.

Brooks, I. (1982) *Where do we go from here?* London: Charles Rapier.

Brown Taylor, B. (1993) Preaching the Body. In O'Day, G. and Long, G. Thomas (eds), *Listening to the Word: Studies in Honor of Fred B. Craddock*. Nashville: Abingdon Press.

Bryan, B. (1998) *A Comparison of Approaches to Teaching English in two Sociolinguistic Environments (Jamaica and London)*. PhD Thesis. London: The UCL Institute of Education.

Bryan, B. (2001) The Role of Linguistic Markers in Manufacturing Consent. In P. Christie (ed.), *Due Respect: Papers on English and English-Related Creoles in the Caribbean in Honour of Professor Robert Le Page*. Mona, Kingston: University of the West Indies Press, pp. 76–96.

Bryan, B. (2010) *Between Two Grammars: Research Practice for Language Learning and Teaching in a Creole-speaking Environment*. Kingston and Miami: Randle.

Butler, A. D. (2007) *Women in the Church of God in Christ: Making a Sanctified World*. Chapel Hill: The University of North Carolina Press.

Buttrick, D. (1986) *Homiletics: Moves and Structures*. Minneapolis, MN: Augsburg Fortress.

Callender, C. and Cameron, D. (1990) Responsive Listening as part of Religious Rhetoric: The Case of Black Pentecostal Preaching. In McGregor, G. and White, R. S. (eds) *Reception and Response: Hearer, Creativity and the Analysis of Spoken and Written Texts*. London: Routledge, pp. 160–78.

Callender, C. (1997) *Education for Empowerment: Practice and Philosophies of Black Teachers*. Stoke-on-Trent: Trentham.

Calley, M. (1965) *God's People. West Indian Pentecostal Sects in England*. Oxford: Oxford University Press.

Carrington, L. D. and Borely, C. (1977) *The Language Arts Syllabus 1975: Comments and Countercomments*. St Augustine, Trinidad: University of the West Indies.

Carrington, L. D. (2001) The Status of Creole in the Caribbean. In P. Christie (ed.) *Due Respect: Papers on English and English-Related Creoles in the Caribbean in Honour of Professor Robert Le Page*. Mona, Kingston: University of the West Indies Press, pp. 24–36.

Channer, Y. (1995) *I am a Promise: The School Achievement of British African Caribbeans*: Stoke-on-Trent: Trentham.

Chimezie, Amuzie (1983) Theories of Black Culture. *The Western Journal of Black Studies*, 7 (4), pp. 216–28.

Christie, P. (1982) *Trends in Jamaican English: Increasing Deviance or Emerging Standards*. Paper presented at the Biennial conference of the Society for Caribbean Linguistics, Suriname.

Christie, P. (ed.) (2001) *Due Respect: Papers on English and English-Related Creoles in the Caribbean in Honour of Professor Robert Le*

Page. Mona, Kingston: University of the West Indies Press, pp. 1–21, 61–78.

Christie, P. (2003) *Language in Jamaica*. Kingston, Jamaica: Arawak.

Clark, K. and Drinkwater, S. (2007) *Ethnic Minorities in the Labour Market: Dynamics and Diversity*. Abingdon: Joseph Rowntree Foundation, Policy Press.

Clifford, J. (1997) *Routes: Travel and Translation in the Late Twentieth Century*. Cambridge, Mass: Harvard University Press.

Cone, J. (1970) *A Black Theology of Liberation*. Maryknoll, New York: Orbis.

Connor, H., Tyers, C., Modood, T. and Hillage, J. (2004) *Why the Difference? A Closer Look at Higher Education Minority Ethnic Students and Graduates. Department for Education and Skills Research* Report 552. London: Department for Education and Skills.

Cooper, C. (2004) *Sound Clash: Jamaican Dancehall Culture at Large*. New York: Palgrave Macmillan.

Cosgrove, Charles H. and W. Dow Edgerton (2007). *In Other Words: Incarnational Translation for Preaching*. Grand Rapids, MI: Eerdmans Publishing.

Craddock, Fred (2001) *As One Without Authority*. Fourth edition (revised). St Louis, Missouri: Chalice Press.

Craig (2006) Teaching English to Jamaican Creole Speakers: A Model of Multi-Dialect Situation. *Language Learning*, 16 (1–2), pp. 9–61.

Dalphinis, M. (1985) *Caribbean and African Languages*. London: Karia Press.

Daniels, D. D. (1999) 'Everybody bids you Welcome': A Multicultural Approach to North American Pentecostalism. In Dempster, M. W. and Petersen D. (eds) *The Globalization of Pentecostalism: A Religion made to Travel*. Carlisle: Regnum and Paternoster, pp. 222–52.

De Camp, D. (1971) The Study of Pidgin and Creole Languages. In Hymes, D. (ed.) *Pidginization and Creolization of Languages*. Cambridge: Cambridge University Press.

Dixon, D. (2014) *The Future of the Past: Forging a Historical Context for Black Gospel Music as a Tradition amongst African Caribbean Pentecostals in Post-war Britain*. PhD Thesis. Birmingham: University of Birmingham.

Douglas, J. Nelson (1981) *For Such a Time as This: The Story of Bishop William J. Seymour and the Azusa Street Revival*. PhD Thesis. Birmingham: University of Birmingham.

Draper, J. and Mtata, M. (2009) Orality, Literature and African Religions www.academia.edu/1502950/Orality_Literature_and_African_Religions_Kenneth_Mtata_and_Jonathan_A._Draper_

Edwards, J. (1992) (ed.) *Let's Praise Him Again*. London: Kingsway.

Edwards, V. K. (1979) *The West Indian Language Issue in British Schools: Challenges and Responses*. London: Routledge and Paul.

Edwards, V. K. (1986) *Language in a Black Community*. Clevedon, Avon: Multilingual Matters.

Edwards, V. K. and Sienkewicz, T. J. (1990) *Oral Cultures Past and Present: Rappin' and Homer*. Oxford: Blackwell.

Erickson, F. (1984) Rhetoric, Anecdote, and Rhapsody: Coherence Strategies in a Conversation among Black American Adolescents. In Tannen, D. (ed.) *Coherence in Spoken and Written Discourse*. Norwood, New Jersey: Ablex, pp. 81–154.

Espinosa, G. (2014) *William J. Seymour and the Origins of Global Pentecostalism: Biography and Documentary History*. Durham, NC and London: Duke University Press.

Fee, G. D. (2006) *Gospel and Spirit: Issues in New Testament Hermeneutics*. Peabody, MA: Hendrickson.

Finnegan, R. (1970) *Oral Literature in Africa*. Oxford: Oxford University Press.

Finnegan, R. (2012) *Oral Literature in Africa*. Cambridge: World Oral Literature Series Volume 1 – Open Book Publishers.

Foster, E. (1992) Women and the Inverted Pyramid of the Black Churches in Britain. In Sahgal, G. and Yuval-Davis, N. (eds) *Refusing Holy Orders*. London: Virago.

Foster, M. (1991) Constancy, Connectedness and Constraints in the lives of African American Teachers. *NWSA Journal* 3 (2), pp. 233–61.

Fryer, P. (1984) *Staying Power: The History of Black People in Britain*. London: Pluto Press.

Gerloff, R. (1992) *A Plea for British Black Theologies: the Black Church Movement in Britain and its transatlantic Cultural and Theological Interaction with Special Reference to the Pentecostal Oneness (Apostolic) and Sabbatarian Movements. Studies in the Intercultural History of Christianity* 2 (77). Frankfurt: Verlag Peter Lang.

Gerloff, R. (2000) An African Continuum in Variation: The African Christian Diaspora in Britain. *Black Theology in Britain: A Journal of Contextual Praxis* (4), pp. 84–112.

Gilbert, K. (2011) *The Journey and Promise of African American Preaching*. Minneapolis: Fortress Press.

Gilkes, C. T. (2001) *If It Wasn't for the Women: Black Women's Experience and Womanist Culture in Church and Community*. Maryknoll, New York: Orbis.

Gillborn, D. (2008) *Racism and Education: Coincidence or Conspiracy*. London: Routledge Falmer.

Goodhew, D. (ed.) (2012) *Church Growth in Britain 1980 to the Present*. Farnham, Surrey: Ashgate.

Good Morning Britain (2018) Piers Morgan interview with Bishop Michael Curry on Tuesday 22 May 2018.

Graves, M. (2006) *The Fully Alive Preacher: Recovering from Homiletical Burnout*. Louisville, KY: Westminster John Knox Press.

Hanson, Drew (27 August 2013) Mahilia Jackson and King's Improvisation in *The New York Times* www.nytimes.com/2013/08/28/opinion/mahalia-jackson-and-kings-rhetorical-improvisation.html

Heller, M. (1988) *Codeswitching: Anthropological and Sociolinguistic Perspectives*. Berlin: Mouton de Gruyter.

Hendriks, H. (2017) Practical theology '[*re*]entering Vernacular Culture?' New Frontiers and Challenges to Doing Theology as Life goes on. *HTS Teologiese Studies/Theological Studies*, 73 (4), pp. 1–10. Open Access: 1–8. www.hts.org.za

Herskovits, M. J. (1958) *The Myth of the Negro Past*. New York: Beacon.

Hewitt, R. (2016) Stealing Land in the Name of Religion: A Rastafari Religio-Political Critique of Land Theft by Global Imperial Forces. *HTS Teologiese Studies/Theological Studies*, 72 (1), pp.1–8.

Hill, C. (1963) *West Indian Migrants and the London Churches*. Oxford: Oxford University Press.

Hollengweger, W. (November 1984) After Twenty Years' Research on Pentecostalism. *Theology* (SPCK) 87:720.

Hollenweger, W. and MacRobert, I. (1988) *The Black Roots and White Racism of Early Pentecostalism in the USA*. London: Macmillan Press.

Hollenweger, W. (1992) The Critical Tradition of Pentecostalism. *Journal of Pentecostal Theology* (1), pp. 7–17.

Hollenweger, W. (1997/2005) *Pentecostalism: Origins and Development Worldwide*. Peabody, Massachusetts: Hendrickson.

Holloway, Joseph (1990) *Africanisms in American Culture*. Bloomington: Indiana.

Holm, J. (1988) *Pidgins and Creoles*. Cambridge: Cambridge University Press.

Holt, G. S. (1972) 'Stylin' outta the Black Pulpit. In Kochman, T. (ed.) *Rapping and Stylin' Out in Urban Black America*. Urbana Champaign: University of Illinois Press, pp. 189–204.

Hopkins, D. N. (1999) *Introducing Black Theology of Liberation*. Maryknoll, New York: Orbis.

Hudson, Lorlett (25 January 2018) Presentation on *Proverbs: Representing Leadership and Cultural Heritage*. Black Theology Forum at Queen's Foundation Birmingham.

Hymes, D. H. (1972) Directions in Sociolinguistics: The Ethnography of Communication. In Gumperz, J. and Hymes, D. (eds) *Models of Interaction of Language and Social Life*. New York: Holt, Rinehart and Winston.

Jackson, L. A. (1986) Proverbs of Jamaica. In Sutcliffe, D. and Wong, A. (eds) *The Language of the Black Experience*. Oxford: Blackwell, pp. 32–6.

Jackson, L. A. (2012) *The Dynamics of Proverbial Sayings: Discover the Connections Within*. Dudley, West Midlands: Arcos.

Jah Bones (1986) Language and Rastafari. In Sutcliffe, D. and Wong, A. (eds) *Language of the Black Experience*. Oxford: Blackwell, pp. 37–51.

Jiménez, P. A. (2015) If You Just Close Your Eyes: Postcolonial Perspectives on Preaching from the Caribbean. *Homiletic*, 40 (1), pp. 22–8.

Johnston, Franklin (2011) *Jamaican Observer*, 23 September. www.jamaicaobserver.com/columns/Lost-in-translation---Is-the-Patois-Bible-a-waste_9769562

Kay, William, K. (2015) The Ecclesial Dimension of Preaching. In Martin, Lee Roy (ed.) *Toward a Pentecostal Theology of Preaching*. Cleveland, TN: CPT Press, pp. 200–15.

Kenyatta, R. G. (2011) *The Journey and Promise of African American Preaching*. Philadelphia: Fortress Press.

Kerswill, P. and Sebba, M. (2011) *From London Jamaican to British Youth Language: The Transformation of a Caribbean Post-Creole Repertoire Into New Multicultural London English*. Paper presented to the Society of Pidgin and Creole Linguists, Accra, Ghana.

Kuck, D. W. (2007) *Preaching in the Caribbean: Building up a People for Mission*. Kingston, Jamaica: Faith Works Press.

Labov, W. (1973) The Logic of nonstandard English. In Keddie, P.N. (ed.) *Tinker, Tailor: The Myth of Cultural Deprivation*. Harmondsworth: Penguin, pp. 21–66.

Lamming, George (1960) *The Pleasures of Exile*. London: Michael Joseph.

Lammy, David (MP) Speech on: *Windrush Migrants in the House of Commons*. Presented on Monday 16 April 2018. Houses of Parliament, Westminster, London.

LaRue, Cleophus J. (2011) *I Believe I'll Testify: The Art of African American Preaching*. Louisville, Kentucky: WJK Press. (Kindle edition).

LaRue, Cleophus J. (2016) *Rethinking Celebration: From Rhetoric to Praise in African American Preaching*. Louisville, Kentucky: WJK Press.

Le Page, R. and D. De Camp (1960) *Jamaican Creole*. London: Macmillan.

Levine, L. W. (1977) *Black Culture and Black Consciousness*. New York: Oxford University Press.

Long, T. G. (2016) *The Witness of Preaching* (third edition). Louisville, KY: Westminister John Knox Press.

Lord, Albert B. (1960) *The Singer of Tales*. Cambridge, MA: Harvard University Press.

MacRobert, I. (1984) *African and European Roots of Black and White Pentecostalism Britain*. Paper presented at the Research Conference on the Pentecostal and Charismatic Movements in Europe. University of Birmingham, 27 and 28 April.

MacRobert, I. (1989) *Black Pentecostalism: Its Origins, Functions and Theology*. Unpublished PhD Thesis. Birmingham: University of Birmingham.

MacRobert, I. (1990) *Black Pentecostalism in Britain: Overt Fundamentalism in Britain: Overt Fundamentalism Versus Implicit Theology*. Draft Chapter.

MacRobert, I. (2003) The Black Roots of Pentecostalism. In West, C. and Claude, Jr. Eddie (eds) *African American Religious Thought: An Anthology*. Louisville: Westminster John Knox Press, pp. 616–28.

Martin, Lee Roy (ed.) (2015) *Toward a Pentecostal Theology of Preaching*. Cleveland, TN: CPT Press.

Mbiti, J. S. (1990) *African Religions and Philosophy*. Portsmouth, New Hampshire: Heinemann.

Mitchell, Henry H. (1970) *Black Preaching*. San Francisco: Eerdmans Publishing Co.

Mitchell, Henry H. (1990) *Black Preaching: The Recovery of a Powerful Art*: Nashville: Abingdon Press.

Mocombe, P. C., and Tomlin, C. (2013) *Language, Literacy and Pedagogy in Postindustrial Societies: The Case of Black Underachievement*. New York: Routledge.

Mocombe, P. C., Tomlin, C. and Wright, C. (2014) *Class Distinctions in the Black Communities: A Racial Caste in Class*. New York: Routledge.

Mocombe, P. C., Tomlin, C. and Showunmi V. (2016) *Jesus and the Street: The Loci of Causality for the Intra-Racial Gender Academic Achievement Gap in Black Urban America and the United Kingdom*. Lanham, MD: University Press of America.

Mocombe, P. C., Tomlin, C. and Callender, C. (2017) *The African-Americanization of the Black Diaspora in Globalization or the Contemporary Capitalist World-System*. Lanham MD: University Press of America.

Morrish, I. (1982) *Obeah, Christ and Rastaman: Jamaica and Its Religion*. Cambridge: Clark and Co.

Muir, D. (2015) *Theological Education and Training among British Pentecostals and Charismatics – A Discussion Paper for CTE*.

Muir, P. E. (2017) Sounds of Blackness? Struggles for Freedom in the

21st-Century. Congregational Songs in South London. In Ackah, W., Dodson, Jualynne E. and Smith, D. R. (eds) *Religion, Culture and Spirituality in Africa and the African Diaspora*. New York/Abingdon, Oxon: Routledge.

Mullings L. J. (2007) Reading Black: Language and Biblical Interpretation in a Black British Context. In Harold Ellens, J. (ed.) *Text and Community: Essays in Memory of Bruce M. Metzger*, Vol. 1. Sheffield: Sheffield Phoenix Press.

Mullings, L. J. (2009, 2010) Teaching Black Biblical Studies in the UK: Special Issues for Consideration and Suggested Hermeneutical Approaches. *Discourse: Learning and Teaching in Philosophical and Religious Studies*, 8 (2), pp. 81–126.

Nelson, D. J. (1981) *For Such a Time as This: The Story of Bishop William J. Symour and the Azusa Street Revival: A Search for Pentecostal/Charismatic Roots*. PhD Thesis. Birmingham: University of Birmingham.

Newton, W. (2016) *The Implications of Harry Emerson Fosdick's Life-Situation Preaching for African-American Preachers*. Doctor of Ministry Thesis. Durham, NC: Divinity School of Duke University.

Nhiwatiwa, E. K. (2012) *How we Preach: Preaching in the African Context*. Nashville, TN: Discipleship Resources International. (Kindle edition)

Okpewho, I. (1992) *African Oral Literature*. Bloomington and Indianapolis: Indiana University Press.

Olofinjana, I. O. (ed.) (2017) *African Voices: Towards African British Theologies*. Carlisle, Cumbria: Langham Global Library.

Olusoga, D. (2016) *Black and British: A Forgotten History*. London: Macmillan.

Oosthuizen, G. C. (1979) *Afro-Christian Religions*. Groningen, Holland: State University of Groningen.

Parry, M. (1930) Studies in the Epic Technique of Oral Verse-Making: I. Homer and Homeric Style. *Harvard Studies in Classical Philology* (41), pp. 73–147.

Peach, C. (1968) *West Indian Migration to Britain: A Social Geography*. London: Oxford University Press for the Institute of Race Relations.

Phillips, M. and Phillips, T. (2009) *Windrush: The Irresistible Rise of Multi-Racial Britain*. London: Harper Collins.

Pollard, V. (1994). *Dread Talk: The Language of Rastafari*. Barbados, Jamaica, Trinidad and Tobago: Canoe Press.

Pollard, V. (2003). *From Jamaican Creole to Standard English*. Mona, Kingston: The University of the West Indies Press.

Pryce, K. (1979) *Endless Pressure*. Harmondsworth: Penguin.

Raboteau, A. (1978) *Slave Religion: The Invisible Institution in the Antebellum South*. Oxford: Oxford University Press.

Rampton, A. (1981) *West Indian Children in Our Schools*. Interim Report of the Committee of Inquiry into the Education of Children from Ethnic Minority Groups. London: HMSO.

Rampton, B. (1995). *Crossings: Language and Ethnicity among Adolescents*. London: Longman.

Reddie, A. (2014) *Black Theology*. London: SCM Press.

Rees, B. and Sherwood, M. (1992) *Black Peoples of the Americas*. Oxford: Heinemann Educational.

Reisman, K. (1974) Contrapuntal Conversations in an Antiguan Village. In Bauman, B. and Sherzer, J. (ed.) *Explorations in the Ethnography of Speaking*. Cambridge: Cambridge University Press.

Rhamie, J. (2007) *Eagles who Soar: How Black Learners find the Path to Success*. Stoke-on-Trent: Trentham.

Rickford, J. R. and Rickford, R. J. (2000) *Spoken Soul: The Story of Black English*. New York: John Wiley and Sons.

Robeck, Jr C. M. (2006) *The Azusa Street Mission & Revival: The Birth of the Classical Pentecostal Movement*. Nashville Tennessee: Thomas Nelson.

Robeck, Jr C. M. and Yong, A. (eds) (2014) *The Cambridge Companion to Pentecostalism*. New York: Cambridge University Press. (Kindle edition)

Roberts, P. (2007). *West Indians and their Language*. Cambridge: Cambridge University Press.

Rollock, N., Gillborn, D., Vincent, C. and Ball, S. J. (2015) *The Colour of Class: The Educational Strategies of the Black Middle Class*. Abingdon, Oxon: Routledge.

Romaine, S. (1988) *Pidgin and Creole Language*. New York: Longman.

Rosen, H. and Burgess T. (1980). *Language and Dialects of London School Children*. London: Ward, Lock Educational.

Rosenberg, B. A. (1988) *Can these Bones Live: The Art of the American Folk Preacher*. Chicago: University Illinois Press.

Sebba, Mark (1993). *London Jamaican*. London: Longman.

Sebba, Mark (2007) Caribbean Creoles and Black English. In Britain, D. (ed.) *Language in the British Isles* (pp. 276–92). Cambridge: Cambridge University Press.

Shields, K. (2002) Crowing Hens are Not Aberrant: Gender, Culture and Performance Conversation. In Mohammed, P. (ed.) *Gendered Realities* (pp. 495–511). Kingston, Jamaica: University of the West Indies Press.

Sindoni, M. G. (2009) Creole in the Caribbean: How Oral Discourse Creates Cultural Identities. *Journal des Africanistes*, 80 (1–2), pp. 217–36.

Smitherman, G. (1977) *Talking and Testifying: The Language of Black America*. Boston: Houghton Mifflin.

Smitherman, G. (1996) *African American English: From the Hood to the Amen Corner.* Bridwell-Bowles, L. and Donehower, K. (eds) University of Minnesota, Centre for Interdisciplinary Studies.

Stevenson, P. K. (2017) *Preaching*. London: SCM Press.

Stewart, C. (2015) *Preparing the Black Church for the 21st Century*. Paper presented at the Black Theological Forum for Queen's Theological Foundation, June.

Sturge, M. (2005) *Look What the Lord Has Done! An Exploration of Black Christian Faith in Britain*. Queensway, Bletchley, MK: Scripture Union.

Sutcliffe, D. (1982) *British Black English*. Oxford: Blackwell.

Sutcliffe, D. (1992) *Systems in Black Language*. Avon, Clevedon: Multilingual Matters.

Sutcliffe, D. and Tomlin, C. (1986) The Black Churches. In Sutcliffe, D. and Wong, A. (eds) *The Language of the Black Experience*. Oxford: Blackwell. pp. 15–31.

Taylor, P. (ed.) (2001) *Nation Dance: Religion, Identity and Cultural Difference in the Caribbean*. Bloomington, Indianapolis: Indiana University Press.

Thomas, F. A. (2016) *Introduction to the Practice of African American Preaching*. Nashville, TN: Abingdon Press.

Thomas, S. (2014) The Lectionary in *The Preachers:* The College of Preachers April.

Thompson, P. (ed.) (2013) *Challenges of Black Pentecostal Leadership in the 21st Century*. London: SPCK.

Todd, L. (1984) *Modern Englishes: Pidgins and Creoles*. London and Oxford: Blackwell.

Tomlin, C. (1988) *Black Preaching Style*. MPhil Thesis. University of Birmingham.

Tomlin, C. (1999) *Black Language Style in Sacred and Secular Contexts*. Medgar Evers College CUNY: Caribbean Diaspora Press.

Tomlin, C. (2014) Black Preaching in *The Preachers*: The College of Preachers. April 153, pp. 5–6.

Tomlin, C. and Bryan, B. (2009) The Writing Performance in English of African Heritage Pupils Two Urban Environments: Birmingham, England and Kingston, Jamaica. *Journal of Education and Development in the Caribbean*. 10 (1), pp. 1–32.

Toulis, N. R. (1997) *Believing Identity: Pentecostalism and the Mediation of Jamaican Ethnicity and Gender in England*. Oxford: Berg.

Trudgill, P. (1990) *Sociolinguistics: An Introduction*. Harmondsworth: Penguin.

Tyson, E. (2013) The Language of Instruction – Jamaican Creole or

Standard English, *The Gleaner*. http://jamaica-gleaner.com/gleaner/20130602/focus/focus4.html

Ukpong, J. S. (2001) Inculturation Hermeneutics: An African Approach to Biblical Interpretation. In Waters, D. and Ulrich, L. (eds) *The Bible in a Word context: An Experiment in Contextual Hermeneutics*. Grand Rapids, MI: Eerdmans, pp. 17–32.

Walls, A. F. (2002) *The Cross-Cultural Process in Christian History*. New York: Orbis Maryknoll.

Walvin, J. (2001) *Black Ivory: A History of British Slavery*. Oxford: Blackwell.

Watson, G. L. (1991) *Jamaican Sayings, Notes on Folklore Aesthetics and Social Control*. Tallahassee: Florida: APM University Press.

Weinreich, U. (1968) *Language in Contact*. The Hague: Mouton.

Wells, J. (1973) *Jamaican Pronunciation in London*. Oxford: Blackwell.

Wilkinson, J. L. (1993) *Church in Black and White: The Black Christian Tradition in 'mainstream' Churches in England. A White Response and Testimony*. Edinburgh: Saint Andrew Press.

Winford, D. (1993) *Predication in Caribbean Creoles*. Amsterdam: John Benjamin.

Winford, D. (1994) Sociolinguistic approaches to language use in the Anglophone Caribbean. In M. Morgan (ed.), *Language and the Social Construction of Identity in Creole Situations*. Los Angeles: Centre for Afro-American Studies, UCLA.

Wolfson, F. (ed.) (1958) *Pageant of Ghana*. Oxford: Oxford University Press.

Xia, Xiufang (2013) Gender Difference in Using Language. *Theory and Practice in Language Studies*, 3 (8), pp. 1485–9.

Yong, A. (April 1999) 'Not Knowing Where The Wind Blows ...' On Envisioning a Pentecostal-Charismatic Theology of Religions. *JPT*, (14), pp. 81–112.

Zeleza, Paul Tiyambe (2006) The Inventions of African Identities and Languages: The Discursive and Developmental Implications. In Selected Proceedings of the 36th *Annual Conference on African Linguistics* (eds) Arasanyin, Olaoba F. and Pemberton, Michael A., 14–26. Somerville, MA: Cascadilla Proceedings Project.

Index of Names and Subjects